Language Arts Grids

Choose & Do

Over 375 Differentiated Activities

- Phonics
- Spelling
- Comprehension
- Word skills
- Writing
- Reference skills

42 grids! 42 practice pages!

Skill practice that gives students choices!

Managing Editor: Jennifer Bragg

Editorial Team: Becky S. Andrews, Diane Badden, Michelle Bayless, Kimberley Bruck, Karen A. Brudnak, Chris Curry, Tazmen Hansen, Marsha Heim, Lori Z. Henry, Debra Liverman, Kitty Lowrance, Laura Mihalenko, Jennifer Nunn, Mark Rainey, Hope Rodgers, Rebecca Saunders, Hope Taylor Spencer, Rachael Traylor, Sharon M. Tresino, Zane Williard

www.themailbox.com

ISBN10 #1-56234-946-5 • ISBN13 #978-1-56234-946-2

Printed in the United States
10 9 8 7 6 5 4 3 2 1

HPS 215489

What's

42 Activity Grids
Nine choices on every grid!

Two simple steps!

1. **Program** the student directions.
2. **Copy** the grid and its practice page.

Plurals

Name ______________________________

Date ________________________

Choose ___ or more activities to do.
When you finish an activity, color its number.

1 List 12 or more items in your classroom. Write the singular and the plural form of each word. Highlight the plural words. desk desks	**2** Copy the list. For each item, roll a die and write the number to tell how many. Change the item to a plural if needed. ___ shelf ___ penny ___ cherry ___ box ___ turkey ___ ox ___ bench ___ wife ___ donkey	**3** Plan a party for your friends. Make a list of ten or more things you will need. Circle each plural word on your list. balloons cake
4 Write a meaning for each word. Use the word's singular form in the meaning. children men mice teeth people feet women sheep deer Children means more than one child.	**5** Do the practice page "Please Feed the Animals."	**6** Look at the words and their plurals. Write two rules for making words that end with *y* plural. toy, toys daisy, daisies tray, trays penny, pennies monkey, monkeys fly, flies
7 Create a song about a farm. Use five or more plural nouns in your song. Make plans to share it with your teacher. Old MacDonald had a farm...	**8** Write the plural of each word. For each word you added *-es* to, draw a picture. fox car pen ball dress cat dish home bag bus peach box	**9** Write directions that tell how to make the words shown plural. Then write the plural form of each word. elf half leaf shelf scarf thief

Choose & Do: Language Arts • ©The Mailbox® Books • TEC61226 • Key p. 91

Note to the teacher: Program the student directions with the number of activities to be completed. Then copy the page and page 24 (back-to-back if desired) for each student. 23

Address different learning levels and styles with a single grid!

Inside

42 Practice Pages

Always activity 5 on the grid

Plurals

Name______________________ Date______________________

Please Feed the Animals

Write the plural form of each animal's name.
Write the word below its rule.

Add *s.*	Add *es.*
Change *y* to *i* and add *es.*	Change *f* to *v* and add *es.*
	Make an irregular plural.

Animals

seal	mouse
wolf	finch
deer	pony
bear	ostrich
bunny	calf
fox	goose
penguin	horse

Choose & Do: Language Arts • ©The Mailbox® Books •

24 **Note to the teacher:** Use with page 23.

Answer Keys on pages 90–96.

Tip!
To save paper, copy a grid and its practice page back-to-back!

Independent practice for

- Morning work
- Guided reading time
- Center work
- Homework
- Free time
- Anytime

Table of Contents

Short and Long Vowels

Name ___________________________

Date ____________________

Choose ___ or more activities to do.
When you finish an activity, color its number.

1 Play I Spy with a partner. Tell in your first clue whether the name of the object you spy has a short- or long-vowel sound.

I spy something with a short-vowel name. It has four legs but does not walk.

2 Add or remove letters to complete the chart.

Short Vowel	Long Vowel
cap	cape
	bead
dim	
got	
	huge
	mane

3 Write eight or more one-syllable action words. Draw a red box around each word with a short-vowel sound. Draw a green line under each word with a long-vowel sound.

4 Softly sing "Five Little Monkeys." Write ten different short-vowel words you hear. Write five different long-vowel words. (Hint: only use one-syllable words.)

5 Do the practice page "Planting Time!"

Lettuce

6 List five short-vowel words. Then rewrite each word by adding *-e* to give it a long-vowel sound. Write a sentence for each pair of words.

kit → kite
I built this kite from a kit.

7 Copy the words. Cut them out. Sort the words by vowel sound (short or long). Glue the groups to another sheet of paper. Label the groups.

peach	red	plum	gray	black
rust	tan	rose	lime	teal

8 Write a different short- or long-vowel word on each of five cards. Draw a picture on a separate card for each word. Swap cards with a classmate and play a memory game on your own.

9 Softly read these words aloud. Write to tell how they are all alike.

wind
lead
read

Note to the teacher: Program the student directions with the number of activities to be completed. Then copy the page and page 6 (back-to-back if desired) for each student.

Short and Long Vowels

Name ______________________ Date ______________

Planting Time!

Use the word bank.
Write each word on its matching row.

short *a*	______	______	long *a*	______	______
short *e*	______	______	long *e*	______	______
short *i*	______	______	long *i*	______	______
short *o*	______	______	long *o*	______	______
short *u*	______	______	long *u*	______	______

Word Bank

plant	crop	shed	leaf	hose
sun	spade	ripe	stem	tube
pack	dry	rain	sod	grow
seed	wilt	mule	pick	mud

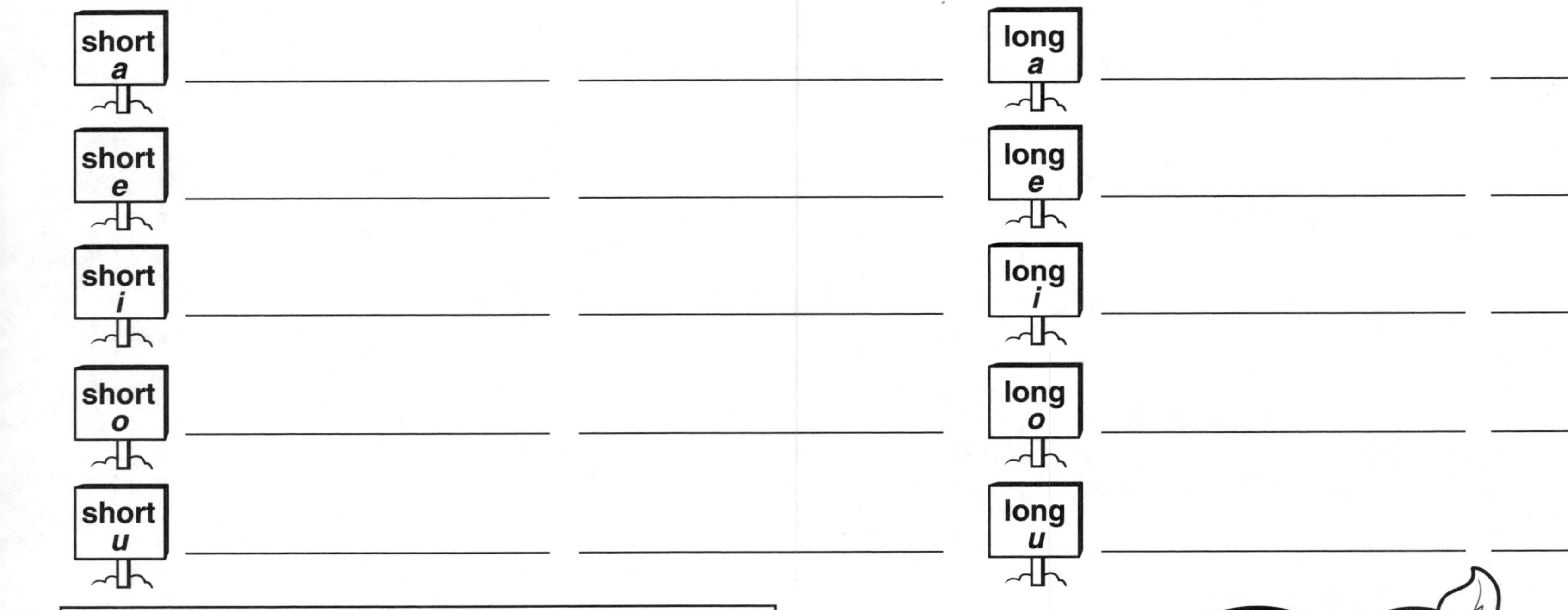

Note to the teacher: Use with page 5.

Word Families

Name ______________________________

Date ____________________

Choose ___ or more activities to do.
When you finish an activity, color its number.

1 Draw a spider. Write the ______ word family on its body. Write a different word from the word family on each leg.	**2** Create a crossword puzzle. Use four or more words from the ______ family and the same number of words from the ______ family.	**3** Make two word lists. Write words from the ______ family in List A. Write words from the ______ family in List B. Then write a silly poem using the *AABB* pattern or the *ABAB* pattern. Use words from the matching lists.
4 Look in books and around the room for five or more words from the ______ family. Write each word you find. Tell where you found it.	**5** Do the practice page "Family Photos."	**6** Work with a partner to list as many words from the ______ family as you can. Check the dictionary and tally a point for each word you spelled correctly. Then make a new list of words from the ______ family.
7 Create five or more fill-in-the-blank sentences. Each blank should be a different word from the ______ family. Make an answer key.	**8** Make a picture dictionary. Use five pages. Draw and label a different word from the ______ family on each page.	**9** List words from the ______ and ______ word families. Copy the chart. Write one word from each list. Tell how the words are alike and different. Repeat three times.

Word	Word	Alike	Different

Note to the teacher: Program the grid's blanks with the word families you wish students to practice. Also program the student directions with the number of activities to be completed. Then copy the page and page 8 (back-to-back if desired) for each student.

Word Families

Name______________________ Date______________

Family Photos

Write each word from the word bank in the matching frame.
Then read each word.

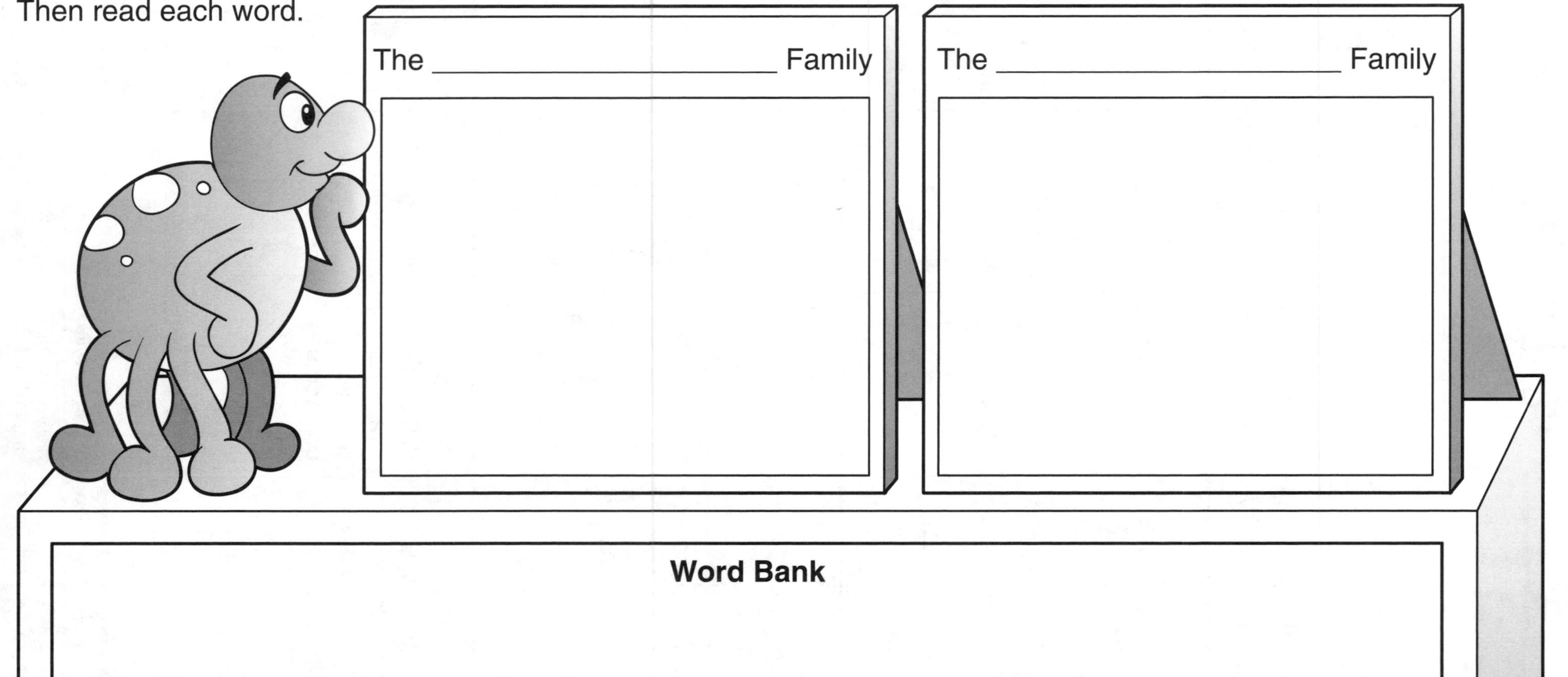

Note to the teacher: Label each picture frame with a different word family. Then write words from both word families in the word bank before copying. Use with page 7.

Beginning Blends With *l* and *r*

Name ________________________________

Date ______________________

bl, cl, fl, gl, pl, sl

br, cr, dr, fr, gr, pr, tr

Choose ___ or more activities to do.
When you finish an activity, color its number.

1 Draw pictures or cut pictures from magazines. Show words with these blends.

br
cr
pr
tr

Glue the pictures to a sheet of paper and label each one.

2 Use a paper clip and pencil to spin the spinner. Write a word for the blend. Repeat nine times.

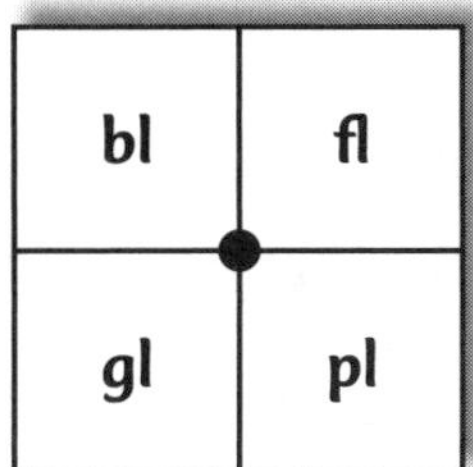

3 Softly sing a song you know well. Make a tally chart to show how many times you hear a word with an *l* blend or an *r* blend.

l blends	
r blends	

4 Use 12 cards. On each card, write a different word that begins with a blend shown.

bl cl fl gl pl

Mix your cards with a partner's set. Use the cards to play Go Fish. Ask for blends.

5 Do the practice page "Lunch on the Fly."

6 Match each blend to each word family. Write each real word you make.

br	**ain**
dr	**ill**
gr	**ook**
tr	**y**

7 Fold a paper to make fourths. Unfold it. In each section, write and illustrate a pair of rhyming words that start with the same letter but have a different blend.

blue, brew	

8 Think of five compound words that have *l* or *r* blends. Draw and label an addition sentence to make each compound word.

9 Find ten or more different words on this page that start with an *l* or *r* blend.

bl, cl, fl, gl, pl
br, cr, fr, dr, pr, tr

Write each word. Trace each blend with a blue crayon.

Note to the teacher: Program the student directions with the number of activities to be completed. Then copy the page and page 10 (back-to-back if desired) for each student.

Beginning Blends With *l* and *r*

Name ______________________ Date ______________

Lunch on the Fly

Complete the puzzle.
Use the word bank.

Across

2. the symbol for addition
3. your parent's father
5. to mix or combine
6. not dirty
7. clothing item a girl might wear
8. smart or showing light

Down

1. a rectangular symbol of a nation
2. a dried plum or to trim a plant
3. happy
4. a pal or buddy
6. a sea animal with a shell
9. a prank

Word Bank

blend bright clean crab dress flag
friend glad grandfather plus prune trick

Note to the teacher: Use with page 9.

Beginning Blends With *s*

Name ______________________________

Date ____________________

Choose ___ or more activities to do.
When you finish an activity, color its number.

1 Write five or more words that start with *sp*. Write a different sentence for each one.

2 Add the blends *sp*, *sk*, and *sc* to each word family. Write each real word.

__in	__are	__an
__ell	__out	__ill
__old	__y	__unk

3 Complete the diagram. Then draw a picture of each word.

4 Choose a blend. Write a tongue twister. Softly read the tongue twister aloud three times. Read it faster each time.

sl
sm
sk

5 Do the practice page "On the Big Screen."

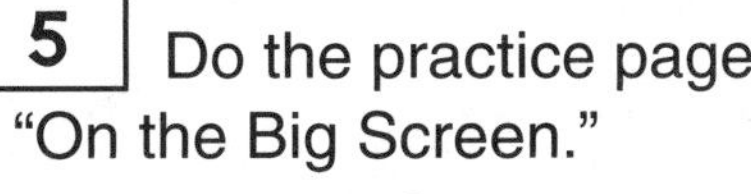

6 Copy the words and cut them out. Sort the words by blends and glue them to another paper. Label each group.

spray	**straw**	**spike**	**stiff**
spend	**stuff**	**stroll**	**spring**

7 Copy the chart. Add six more science words. Start each word with the blends shown.

snail	space	stem
sn	sp	st
sn	sp	st

8 Draw a picture of a word that begins with *scr*, *spr*, or *str*. Write the word under the picture, leaving blanks for the three-letter blend. Repeat seven more times. Have a friend fill in the blanks.

9 Write *stop* down your paper. Circle it. Write a word that has an *s* blend across each row.

Note to the teacher: Program the student directions with the number of activities to be completed. Then copy the page and page 12 (back-to-back if desired) for each student.

Beginning Blends With *s*

Name______________________________ Date____________________

On the Big Screen

Underline the beginning blend of each word in the word bank.
Circle each word in the puzzle.

Word Bank

scare	scream	screen	skin	slime
smart	smoke	snack	spoke	spray
sprint	stare	stripe	strong	sweet

t	h	s	c	r	e	a	m	o	s	k	b	s	d
w	s	p	r	i	n	t	r	c	l	s	j	w	s
t	x	y	s	b	d	z	v	h	i	p	g	e	t
r	s	u	c	a	f	l	q	r	m	o	c	e	r
s	m	a	r	t	s	w	l	u	e	k	a	t	i
t	o	z	e	l	l	g	s	o	v	e	r	s	p
r	k	n	e	d	s	s	t	q	c	e	h	t	e
o	e	s	n	a	c	k	i	w	u	m	p	a	x
n	h	w	j	v	a	i	n	y	x	c	b	r	p
g	a	c	y	s	r	n	s	e	k	f	j	e	o
r	z	t	k	n	e	l	u	m	s	p	r	a	y

 Note to the teacher: Use with page 11.

Consonant Digraphs

Name ______________________________

Date ____________________

Choose ___ or more activities to do.
When you finish an activity, color its number.

1 List five words that begin with *th.* List five words that end with *th.* Use the words to play a game of Hangman with a partner.	**2** Make a word search that has eight words that start with *wh.*	**3** Create a picture dictionary with five or more pages. Write a different word that begins with *ch* on each page and draw its picture. cheese
4 Write a tongue twister. Use as many words that start with *sh* as you can. Write another tongue twister using words that start with *ch.* Softly read your tongue twisters aloud.	**5** Do the practice page "Give a Cheer." GO TEAM!	**6** Write a word that ends with *ch, sh,* or *th* on a card. Draw a matching picture. Write a riddle on the other side of the card. Make six cards in all.
7 Draw a simple shape on a sheet of paper and cut it out. Place the leftover frame atop a page in a textbook. Copy every word in that space that starts or ends with *ch, sh, th,* or *wh.* Softly read the word list aloud. Repeat with another textbook page.	**8** Write a story. Use as many words as you can that end with *ch, sh,* or *th.* Highlight each word.	**9** Plan a cheer that uses words that begin with *wh.* Make plans with your teacher to share your cheer with the class. Let's go, w-h!

Note to the teacher: Program the student directions with the number of activities to be completed. Then copy the page and page 14 (back-to-back if desired) for each student.

Consonant Digraphs

Name ______________________ Date ____________

Give a Cheer

Add *ch, sh, th,* or *wh* to make a word.
Write the new word on the matching pom-pom.

Note to the teacher: Use with page 13.

Vowel Diphthongs

Name ______________________________

Date ____________________

Choose ___ or more activities to do.
When you finish an activity, color its number.

1 Copy the words shown. Cut out the words, sort them by spelling *(oi* and *oy),* and glue them to another sheet of paper. Label each group.

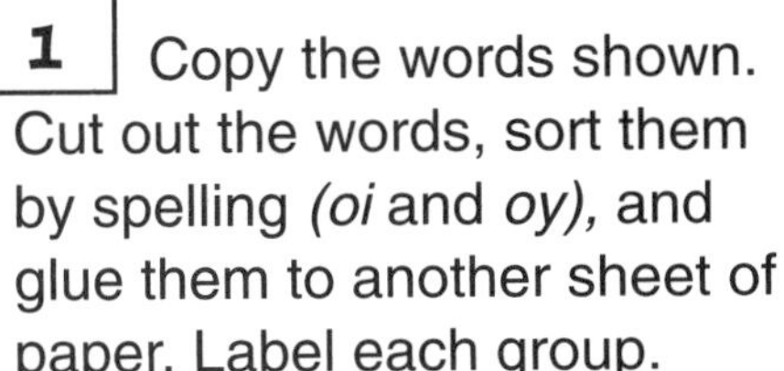

2 Write four sentences. In each sentence, use two words spelled with *oo* that have different sounds. Underline each *oo* word.

The ice pack soothed my sore foot.

3 List rhyming words for each word shown. Use the *ow* spelling in each rhyming word. Then softly read your lists aloud.

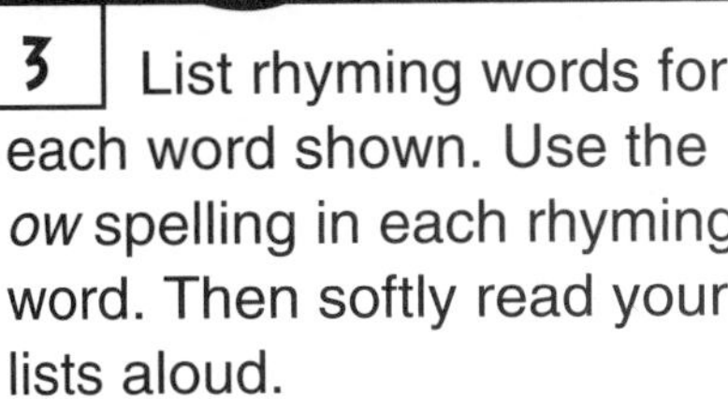

4 Look at each set of letters. Add *au* or *aw.* Write the words.

au	
cght	tumn
gust	to
vlt	becse

aw	
str	ls
hk	dr
cl	yn

5 Do the practice page "In Bloom."

6 Make a picture and word quiz. Use words spelled with *oi* and *oy.* Then make an answer key. Have a friend take your quiz.

7 Write *soon.* Change one letter to make a new word. Keep *oo* in each word. After you list all the words you can, draw a ☾ next to each word that has the same *oo* sound as in *moon.*

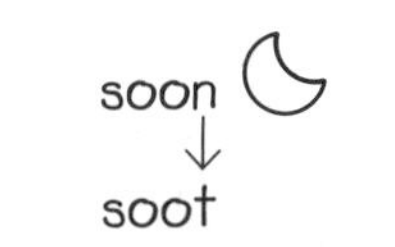

8 Copy the words. Write *ou* or *ow* to fill in each blank. Use a brown crayon to trace the words spelled with *ow.*

p__der sh__er sn__t

d__n tr__t cl__d

fl__er b__nce cr__d

9 Create a poster. On one side, show words spelled with *aw.* On the other side, show words spelled with *au.*

Note to the teacher: Program the student directions with the number of activities to be completed. Then copy the page and page 16 (back-to-back if desired) for each student.

Vowel Diphthongs

Name ____________________ Date ____________

In Bloom

Write *oo, oi,* or *oy* to complete each word in the word bank.
Copy each word onto the matching flower.

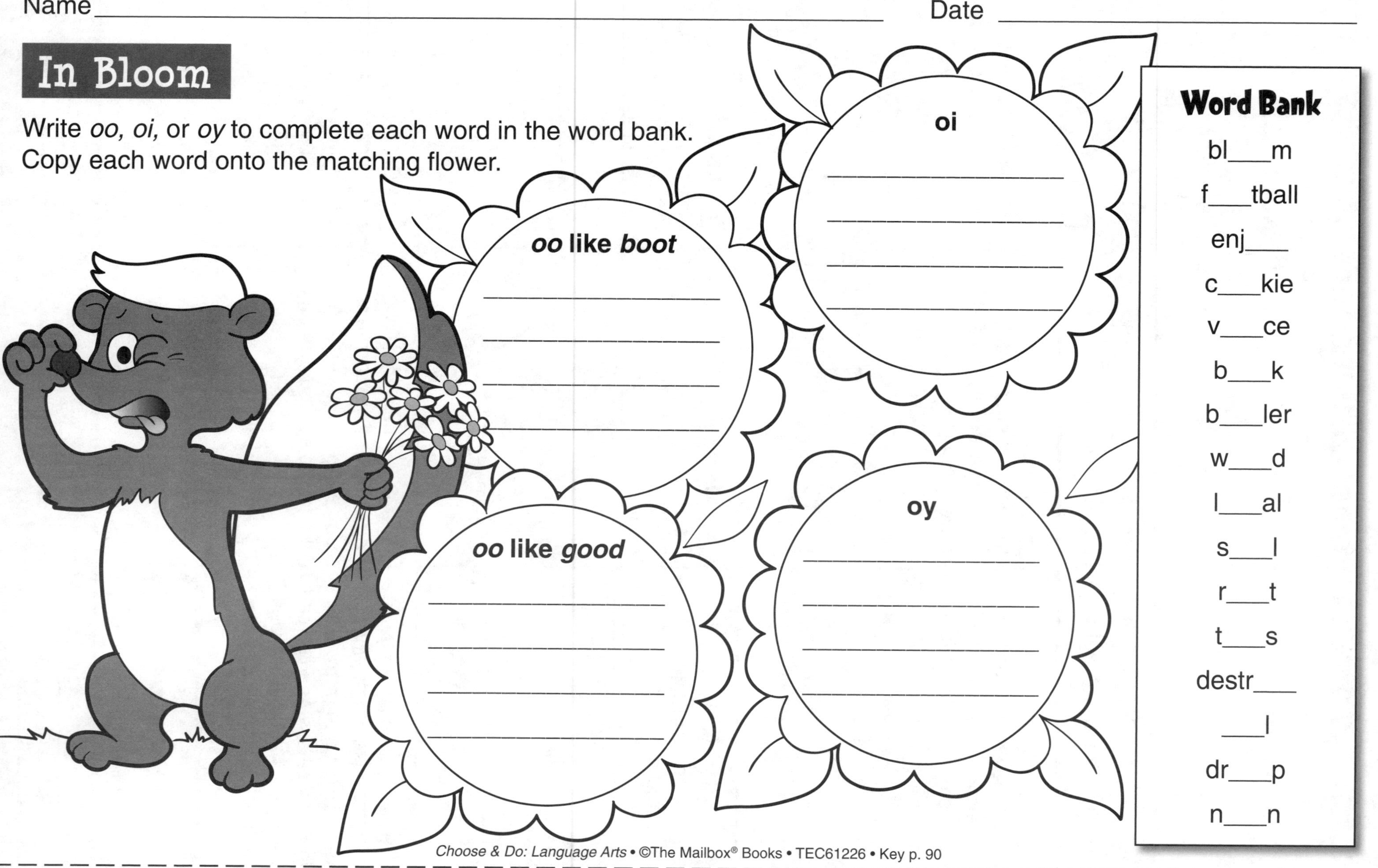

Word Bank

bl___m
f___tball
enj___
c___kie
v___ce
b___k
b___ler
w___d
l___al
s___l
r___t
t___s
destr___
___l
dr___p
n___n

Note to the teacher: Use with page 15.

Spelling Patterns: Long Vowels *a* and *i*

Name ______________________________

Date ____________________

Choose ___ or more activities to do.
When you finish an activity, color its number.

1 Write the days of the week. Circle the two letters in each word that make the long *a* sound. Write seven more words with the same spelling pattern.

2 Draw a train. Write on each car a word spelled with *ai*. Add as many cars to the train as you can.

3 Copy each word. Trace the letters that make the long *a* and long *i* sounds. Then write three rhyming words with the same pattern for each word.

cake	**skate**	**blame**	**whale**
chase	**price**	**smile**	**ride**

4 Write six words spelled with *igh* to complete the word web. Then write each word in a sentence.

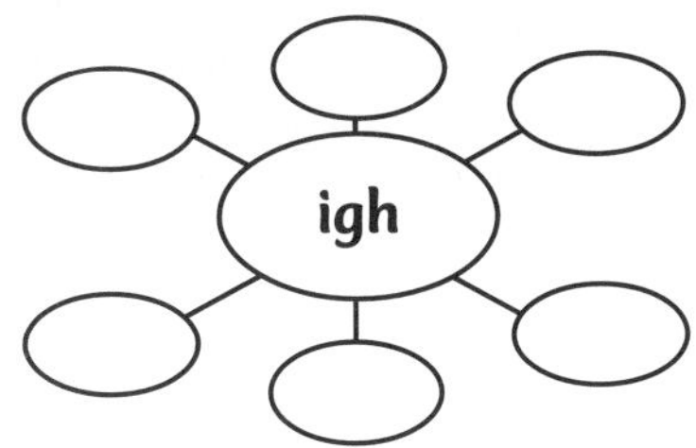

5 Do the practice page "A Lengthy Project."

6 Add one letter to each word to give the word a long *a* sound.

bat	**mad**	**mat**	**pal**
pad	**gal**	**cap**	**tap**
man	**fat**	**lad**	**rad**

7 Softly read the sentence aloud. Make a plan to tell your teacher how the underlined words are alike and different.

<u>I</u> tossed a <u>pie</u> <u>high</u> in the <u>sky</u>.

8 Match each beginning sound with the ending *y* or *ie* to make real words.

sp	**t**	**wh**
fl	**l**	**p**
tr	**b**	**d**

9 Write a list of words with long *i* spellings. Then use your finger to write each word on the carpet or on your backpack.

Note to the teacher: Program the student directions with the number of activities to be completed. Then copy the page and page 18 (back-to-back if desired) for each student.

Spelling Patterns: Long Vowels *a* and *i*

Name ________________________ Date ____________

A Lengthy Project

Write a word to name each picture.
Add or subtract letters to make a new word.

1. 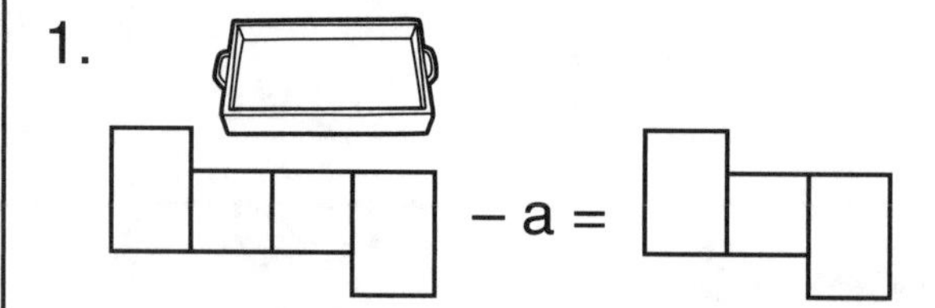
   □□□□ – a = □□□

2. 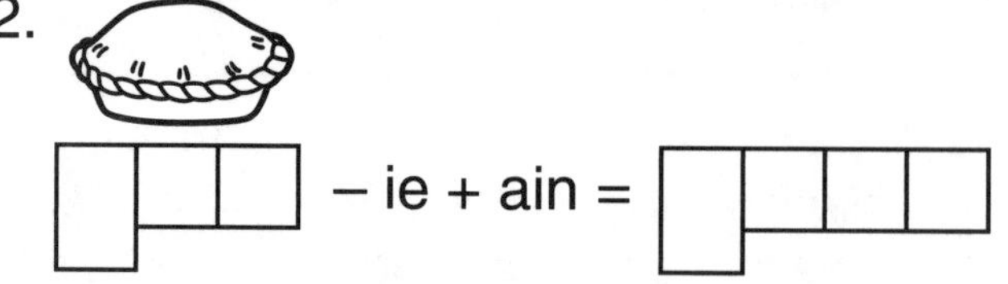
   □□□ – ie + ain = □□□□

3. 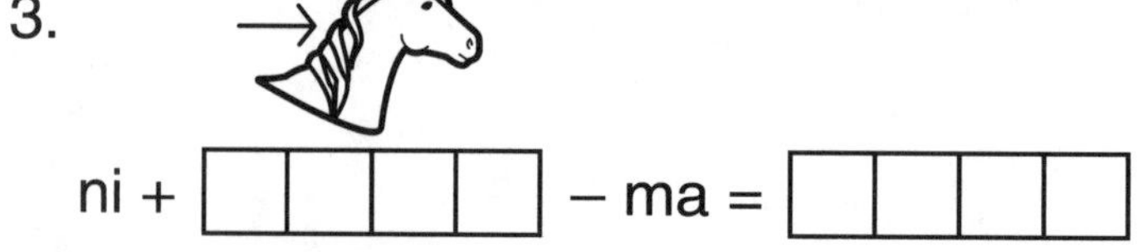
   ni + □□□□ – ma = □□□□

4. 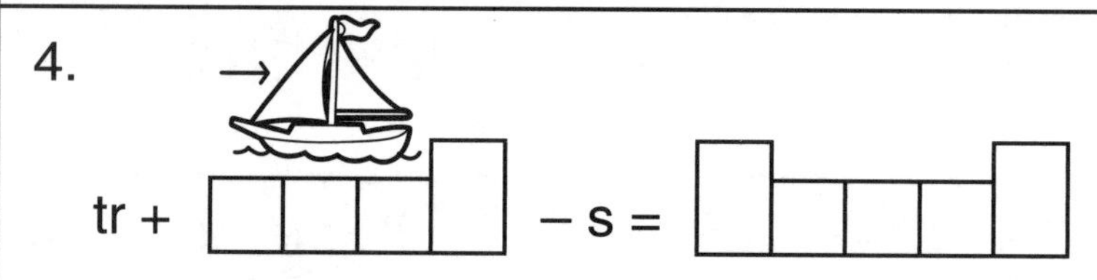
   tr + □□□□ – s = □□□□□

5. 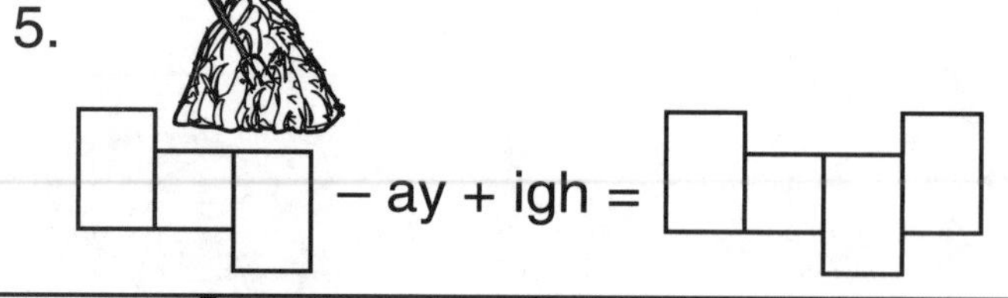
   □□□ – ay + igh = □□□□

6. 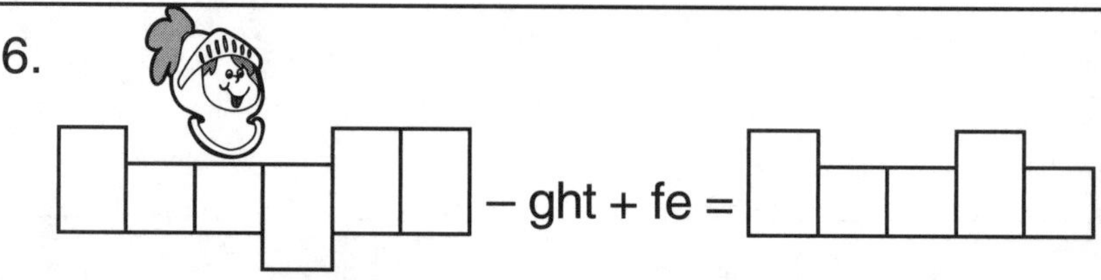
   □□□□□□ – ght + fe = □□□□□

7.
   fa + □□□□ – di = □□□□

8. 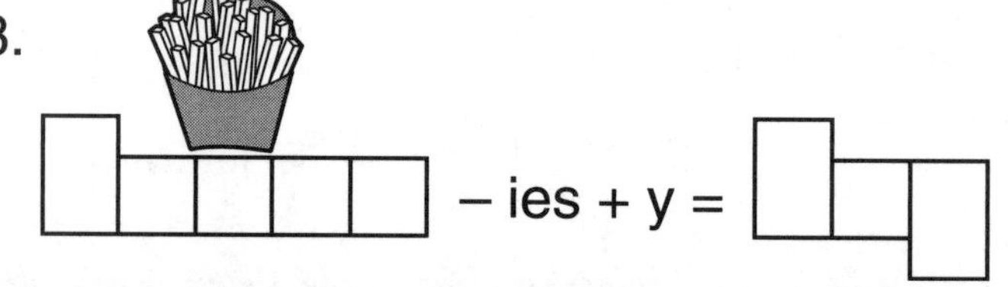
   □□□□□ – ies + y = □□□

 Note to the teacher: Use with page 17.

Spelling Patterns: Long Vowels *e* and *o*

Name ______________________________

Date ________________________

Choose ___ or more activities to do.
When you finish an activity, color its number.

1 Quietly sing "Row, Row, Row Your Boat." Write two words from the song with the long *o* sound and two words with the long *e* sound. Make your own song that uses words with these long vowel sounds.	**2** Copy the tree. Write a word or name on each leaf that uses the long *e* spelling pattern on its branch. ee ea	**3** Add one letter to each word to make a new word with a long *e* or long *o* spelling. mop net cot set hop ten got red cop fed
4 Copy each word. If the *y* at the end of the word makes the long *e* sound, trace the word with a green crayon. very spy every try dirty sorry baby family dry study	**5** Do the practice page "A Dirty Chimney."	**6** Play tic-tac-toe with a friend. Instead of an *X,* Player 1 writes a word with a long *o* spelling in each space. Instead of an *O,* Player 2 writes a word with a long *e* spelling in each space.
7 Write a word with a long *o* spelling. Use a letter from the end of the word to start another word with a long *o* spelling. Circle each word. Continue as long as you can. c o a t o a s t o a d	**8** Copy the long *e* wheel. Write two words for each spelling pattern. 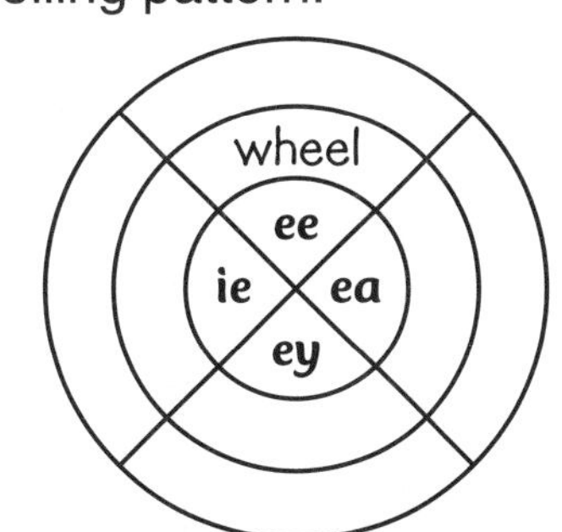	**9** List 12 or more words that end with *ow.* Quietly read the list aloud. Cross out any words that do not have the long *o* sound.

Note to the teacher: Program the student directions with the number of activities to be completed. Then copy the page and page 20 (back-to-back if desired) for each student.

Name ______________________ Date ______________

A Dirty Chimney

Write *ea, ee, ow,* or *oa* to complete each word.
Trace each brick by the code.

 Note to the teacher: Use with page 19.

Inflectional Endings: *-ed, -ing*

Name ____________________________

Date ________________________

Choose ___ or more activities to do.
When you finish an activity, color its number.

1 Write a journal entry telling what you did yesterday. Circle each word that ends with *-ed* or *-ing*.

2 Copy and complete the chart.

Base Word	Past	Present
		is raining
	washed	
learn		
		is cleaning
spell		

3 Work with a partner. Take turns saying a sentence that uses one word from each column.

am	listening
was	playing
is	calling
are	watching

4 Finish each sentence. Use a verb that ends in *-ed*.

Yesterday __________.
Last year __________.
Three days ago __________.

5 Do the practice page "Colorful Science."

6 Copy the verbs. Cross out each verb that cannot have an *-ed* ending.

brush	color	eat	say
find	fold	know	walk
laugh	see	sing	think
play	sleep	snow	buy

7 Draw six pictures of things you like to do. Write a verb that describes each picture. Write the past tense and future tense of each verb.

bake baked will bake

8 Write three or more sentences about the weather. Use a different word from below in each sentence.

rain	rained	raining
snow	snowed	snowing

9 Make a poster to help your classmates add *-ed* or *-ing* to base words. Show which letters they should take away and which letters they should double.

Note to the teacher: Program the student directions with the number of activities to be completed. Then copy the page and page 22 (back-to-back if desired) for each student.

Inflectional Endings: *-ed, -ing*

Name ____________________ Date ____________

Colorful Science

Write each new word.
Color the beaker by the code.

Color Code

red = no change; add *-ed* or *-ing*
blue = drop the *e;* add *-ed* or *-ing*
yellow = double the consonant; add *-ed* or *-ing*

1 turn + ing = ________	9 lift + ed = ________
2 write + ing = ________	10 sit + ing = ________
3 bat + ed = ________	11 look + ed = ________
4 plant + ed = ________	12 think + ing = ________
5 swim + ing = ________	13 drive + ing = ________
6 sing + ing = ________	14 win + ing = ________
7 hope + ing = ________	15 close + ed = ________
8 type + ed = ________	16 walk + ed = ________

Note to the teacher: Use with page 21.

Plurals

Name ______________________________

Date ____________________

Choose ___ or more activities to do.
When you finish an activity, color its number.

1 List 12 or more items in your classroom. Write the singular and the plural form of each word. Highlight the plural words.

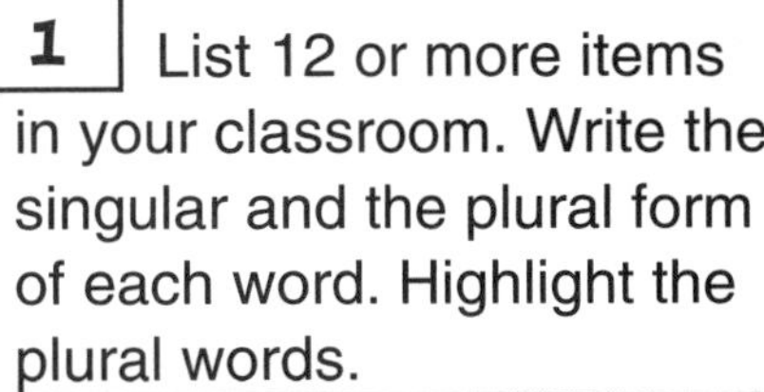

desk desks

2 Copy the list. For each item, roll a die and write the number to tell how many. Change the item to a plural if needed.

___ **shelf**	___ **penny**	___ **cherry**
___ **box**	___ **turkey**	___ **ox**
___ **bench**	___ **wife**	___ **donkey**

3 Plan a party for your friends. Make a list of ten or more things you will need. Circle each plural word on your list.

balloons

cake

4 Write a meaning for each word. Use the word's singular form in the meaning.

children	**men**	**mice**
teeth	**people**	**feet**
women	**sheep**	**deer**

Children means more than one child.

5 Do the practice page "Please Feed the Animals."

6 Look at the words and their plurals. Write two rules for making words that end with *y* plural.

toy, toys	**daisy, daisies**
tray, trays	**penny, pennies**
monkey, monkeys	**fly, flies**

7 Create a song about a farm. Use five or more plural nouns in your song. Make plans to share it with your teacher.

8 Write the plural of each word. For each word you added *-es* to, draw a picture.

fox	**car**	**pen**
ball	**dress**	**cat**
dish	**home**	**bag**
bus	**peach**	**box**

9 Write directions that tell how to make the words shown plural. Then write the plural form of each word.

elf	**half**
leaf	**shelf**
scarf	**thief**

Note to the teacher: Program the student directions with the number of activities to be completed. Then copy the page and page 24 (back-to-back if desired) for each student.

Name ______________________ Date ______________

Please Feed the Animals

Write the plural form of each animal's name.
Write the word below its rule.

Add *s*.	Add *es*.
Change *y* to *i* and add *es*.	Change *f* to *v* and add *es*.
	Make an irregular plural.

Animals

seal	mouse
wolf	finch
deer	pony
bear	ostrich
bunny	calf
fox	goose
penguin	horse

 Note to the teacher: Use with page 23.

Homophones

Name ______________________________

Date ______________________

Choose ___ or more activities to do.
When you finish an activity, color its number.

1 List five homophone pairs. Then use each pair of words in a different sentence. Underline each homophone.

rode, road

I <u>rode</u> my scooter next to the <u>road</u>.

2 Make a ten-sentence homophone quiz. Include an answer key.

3 Use the wrong homophone in a silly sentence. Draw a picture to go with it. Repeat the steps three more times.

Dad placed the golf ball on the tea.

4 Write a riddle question for each answer.

sun's son **bored board**
male's mail **hoarse horse**

What do you call a faded bucket? a pale pail

5 Do the practice page "Buried Bones."

6 Read this sentence aloud. Replace each word with its homophone. Write the new sentence. Draw a picture to match.

Eye sea sum aunts buy hour blew flours.

7 Create a homophone crossword puzzle. Use one homophone for the clue and the other for the answer.

8 Make a game for practicing homophones. Play your game with a partner.

bail
bale
steak

9 Write a homophone for each contraction.

we've
we'll
we'd
they're
you're
I'll
who's

Note to the teacher: Program the student directions with the number of activities to be completed. Then copy the page and page 26 (back-to-back if desired) for each student.

Homophones

Name ______________________ Date ______________

Buried Bones

For each word below, circle a homophone in the story.
Write the circled word beside its homophone.

1. fined	____________	7. knows	____________
2. four	____________	8. sale	____________
3. grate	____________	9. seize	____________
4. herd	____________	10. tail	____________
5. hi	____________	11. wood	____________
6. lead	____________	12. ewe	____________

Have you ever heard the tale of Captain Ruff? He was a great and daring pirate. He and his crew would sail the high seas. They were looking for fortunes. They never did find much gold. But Captain Ruff always followed his nose. It led him to many tasty treasures!

Note to the teacher: Use with page 25.

Spelling

Use with your own word list.

Name ____________________________

Date ________________________

Choose ___ or more activities to do.
When you finish an activity, color its number.

1 Hide all of your spelling words in a word search. Then solve it.	**2** Say a spelling word. Then use one finger to spell the word on the back of your other hand. Say each letter aloud as you write it. Repeat with each of your spelling words.	**3** Copy the chart. In the first column, write each spelling word. Then complete the second column. Word | Number of Vowels
4 Create a poem. Include six or more of your spelling words in the poem.	**5** Do the practice page "A Clever Cowboy."	**6** Write each word one letter at a time. Then draw lines to make steps. d d r d r a d r a w
7 Make up a cheer to help you remember how to spell three or more of your longer spelling words. Use body movements. Make plans to share your cheer with the class.	**8** For each spelling word, write a question that includes the word.	**9** Decorate eight or more of your spelling words to show their meanings. cloudy c l i m b rabbit

Note to the teacher: Each student needs a list of eight or more spelling words. Program the student directions with the number of activities to be completed. Then copy the page and page 28 (back-to-back if desired) for each student.

Name ______________________ Date ______________________

A Clever Cowboy

Write each spelling word three times.
Count the syllables in the word.
Circle the word in the matching column.

1	2	3 or more
rodeo	rodeo	(rodeo)

 Note to the teacher: Use with page 27.

Spelling

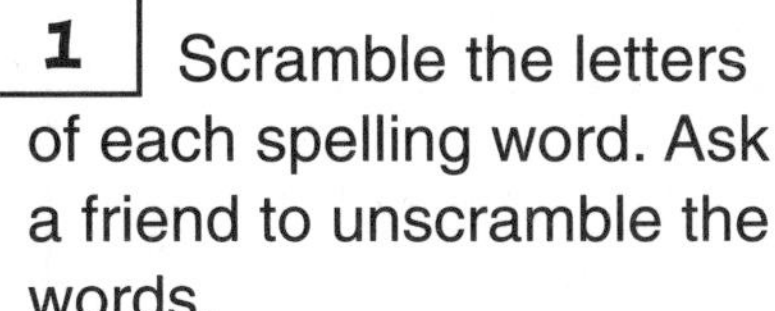

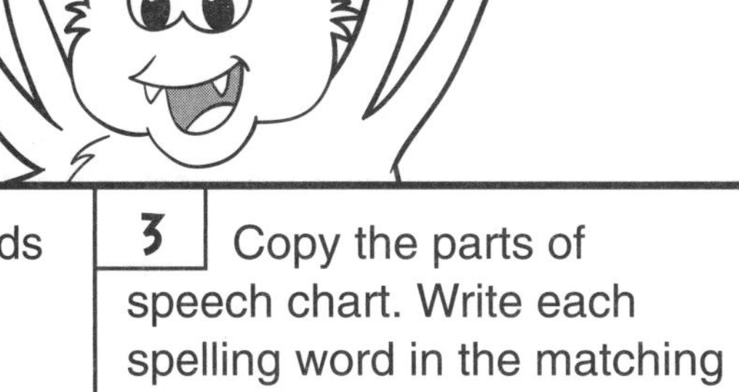

Name ______________________________

Date ______________________

Choose ___ or more activities to do.
When you finish an activity, color its number.

1 Scramble the letters of each spelling word. Ask a friend to unscramble the words.

2 List your spelling words in **reverse** ABC order.

3 Copy the parts of speech chart. Write each spelling word in the matching space or spaces.

Nouns	Verbs
Adjectives	**Other**

4 Create a description for each of your spelling words.

spider: This word has six letters. It has a long vowel and it starts with a consonant blend. It ends with -er.

5 Do the practice page "A Painting Pro."

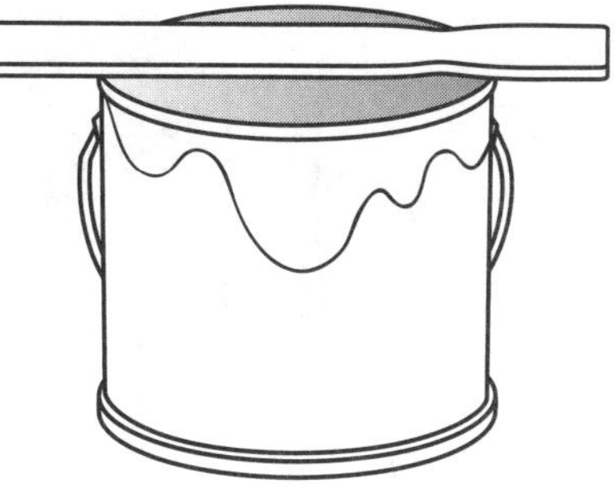

6 Write each of your spelling words. Use the code.

a = ☆ o = ♔
e = ☺ u = △
i = ☒

p☆☒nt

7 Look at your spelling list. Write to describe any letter patterns you see. Write three or more new words that would fit in a letter pattern.

8 Spell your words aloud. Show the hand signal for each letter.

tall letters = (like *b, d, f*)

short letters = (like *a, c, e*)

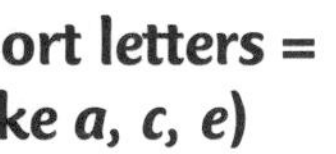

hanging letters = (like *g, j, p*)

9 Pair each of your spelling words with another word on your list. Write each pair of words in a sentence.

brush, trash

The painter puts the brush in the trash.

Note to the teacher: Each student needs a list of eight or more spelling words. Program the student directions with the number of activities to be completed. Then copy the page and page 30 (back-to-back if desired) for each student.

Name ____________________ Date ____________

A Painting Pro

Write each spelling word on the matching paint can.

Hint: some words may be written on more than one can, and some words may not be written at all.

Words With Two Syllables

Words With Long Vowels

Words With More Than Six Letters

Words With Silent Letters

The First Five Words in ABC Order

Words With Two Vowels

Note to the teacher: Use with page 29.

Main Idea and Details

Name ______________________________

Date ________________________

Choose ___ or more activities to do.
When you finish an activity, color its number.

1 Draw a food that you like. Write three details that tell why you like it.	**2** Copy one main idea from below. Write four details that support the idea. **Plants have needs.** **School is important.** **Kittens are cute.**	**3** Draw the web shown. Copy the main idea. In each circle draw a detail that tells about the main idea. **a happy day**
4 Softly read a paragraph aloud. Write the main idea. List two details from the paragraph that tell about the main idea.	**5** Do the practice page "A Beautiful Bloom."	**6** Write to tell why a reader should know the difference between a main idea and a detail. Share your reasons with a friend.
7 Write a paragraph. Tell about one of your hobbies. **Sentence 1: Name the hobby.** **Sentences 2–4: Give details about the hobby.** **Sentence 5: Tell how you feel about the hobby.**	**8** Draw what could be the main idea for the listed details. Then rewrite the details to make them more exact. • **colorful** • **very fast** • **expensive**	**9** Write a topic sentence for the main idea below. Then write three details that support the main idea. **I know a person who is funny.**

Note to the teacher: Program the student directions with the number of activities to be completed. Then copy the page and page 32 (back-to-back if desired) for each student.

Main Idea and Details

Name ______________________ Date ______________________

A Beautiful Bloom

Read a story.
Complete the chart.

 Note to the teacher: Use with page 31.

Fact and Opinion

Name ______________________________

Date ______________________

Choose ___ or more activities to do.
When you finish an activity, color its number.

1 Think about something you read yesterday. Write three facts and three opinions about the topic.	**2** Copy the sentences. Tell whether each is a fact or an opinion and explain why. **The cheetah is the fastest land animal.** **A cheetah has beautiful fur.**	**3** Draw a sketch of your classroom. Write five facts about the room.
4 Create a song about a cereal you like to eat. Put two or more facts and two or more opinions in your song. Toasted O's are round and yummy. They feel good inside my tummy.	**5** Do the practice page "Fast Food."	**6** Ask six friends about today's school lunch. Write their opinions. MILK
7 Pretend you are writing a biography about a famous person. List eight questions you can ask to learn facts about the person. • Where was the person born?	**8** Make a poster about a movie you like. On the poster, write three facts and three opinions about the movie. It's the best cartoon of the year!	**9** Write a newspaper story about a team's winning game. Put five or more facts in your story. Underline each fact.

Note to the teacher: Program the student directions with the number of activities to be completed. Then copy the page and page 34 (back-to-back if desired) for each student.

Fact and Opinion

Name ______________________________ Date ______________________

Fast Food

Read each sentence.
Color the paw in the matching column.

	Fact	Opinion
1. Cheetahs are the finest wildcats.	Y	A
2. Cheetahs live mainly in the African grasslands.	L	B
3. A cheetah's spots help it hide in tall, dry grass.	N	Q
4. A cheetah can run up to 70 miles per hour.	E	J
5. Male cheetahs live by themselves or with a small group.	G	U
6. It is thrilling to watch a cheetah chase its prey!	X	S
7. Cheetahs have sharp eyesight.	O	K
8. Most cheetah mothers have three to five cubs in each litter.	H	I
9. Cheetah cubs are so cute!	C	Z
10. There may only be about 12,000 cheetahs left in the wild.	R	D
11. People should take better care of the cheetahs' home.	V	T
12. It would be sad if cheetahs were extinct.	W	P

What are three animals that cheetahs hunt?
To find out, write each colored letter from above on the matching numbered line or lines below.

__ __ __ __ __ __ __ __ __ ,
1 3 11 4 2 7 12 4 6

__ __ __ __ __ __ __ __ ,
5 1 9 4 2 2 4 6

and __ __ __ __ __
8 1 10 4 6

 Note to the teacher: Use with page 33.

Cause and Effect

Name ______________________________

Date ______________________

Choose ___ or more activities to do.
When you finish an activity, color its number.

1 Create a funny story telling people what could happen if they leave the front door open. ...then a hippo came in because the door was open.	**2** Make a cause-and-effect chain with ten links. The sentence on each link is an effect of the link before. I fell on the ice. ↓ I broke my leg. ↓ I couldn't play soccer. ↓	**3** Draw a picture that shows three or more causes and their effects. Write about your picture. The cat's tail hurts because it is stuck.
4 Write three causes and effects from your favorite fairy tales. Draw a picture to go with each cause and effect. Cinderella lost her slipper because she ran away.	**5** Do the practice page "At the Zoo."  	**6** Write six sentences that each have a cause and an effect. In each sentence, write the effect before the cause. I was happy because I won the race.
7 List six or more possible causes for the effect below. **Effect: My family was very proud of me.**	**8** Make a cause-and-effect matching game. Make plans to play the game with a friend.	**9** Create a timeline of five things that happened yesterday. Write a sentence telling the cause or effect of each event. 9:00 I got an *A* on my spelling test because I studied.

Note to the teacher: Program the student directions with the number of activities to be completed. Then copy the page and page 36 (back-to-back if desired) for each student.

Cause and Effect

Name ______________________ Date ______________________

At the Zoo

Read the story.

We are going to the zoo because the museum is closed. My brother likes tigers, so we go to see the cats first. Then we walk to see the elephants. It is hot, and the elephants are spraying themselves with water. Since we brought our lunches, we sit down to have a picnic. It is also time to feed the seals, so a crowd gathers to watch. Soon we hear a group of children laughing. They are laughing because some monkeys are doing tricks. Finally, it is time for us to go home.

Complete the chart.

Cause	Effect
	We are going to the zoo.
My brother likes tigers.	
It is hot.	
	We have a picnic.
	A crowd gathers to watch.
Some monkeys are doing tricks.	

Compare and Contrast

Name ______________________________

Date ________________________

Choose ___ or more activities to do.
When you finish an activity, color its number.

1 Choose two book characters. Make a T chart. Write three ways the characters are alike and three ways they are different.

Alike	Different

2 Compare the events of today to the events of yesterday. Make a list of all the ways the two days are the same.

3 Copy and complete the topic sentence. Then write three or more sentences to finish the paragraph.

________ and ________ are different in many ways.

4 Draw a picture of yourself. Share your picture with a classmate who also drew a picture. Talk about ways your pictures are alike and different. Keep a list of the things you talk about.

5 Do the practice page "Lovely Fliers."

6 Design two ads, each for a different brand of toothpaste. Include details so that a shopper looking at both ads can find three ways the toothpastes are the same and three ways they are different.

7 Copy the chart. Write a different food at the top of the second and third column. Use check marks to complete the chart.

healthy		
tasty		
messy		
served hot		

8 Write a letter to your principal. Compare and contrast your two favorite things about school. Underline ways they are alike with a blue crayon and underline ways they are different with a red crayon.

9 Write five riddles that compare and contrast two different things. Write the answers.

1. Both are flying insects. One has a thin body, and the other has a fat body.

   Answer: butterfly and moth

Note to the teacher: Program the student directions with the number of activities to be completed. Then copy the page and page 38 (back-to-back if desired) for each student.

Compare and Contrast

Name ______________________ Date ____________

Lovely Fliers

Read.
Complete the diagram.

Bev Butterfly and Mia Moth are flying insects. Each one has two pairs of wings that are covered with scales. You might find Bev or Mia flying near a flower garden because they both help pollinate flowers. But the chances that you would see them there at the same time are pretty slim. Why? Bev likes to fly during the day, while Mia prefers to fly at night. How else might you tell them apart? Bev has a slim body, and Mia has a plump body. There are knobs at the ends of Bev's antennae but not Mia's. When Bev rests, she holds her wings up. When Mia rests, she spreads her wings out flat. Do you think you could tell these two insects apart?

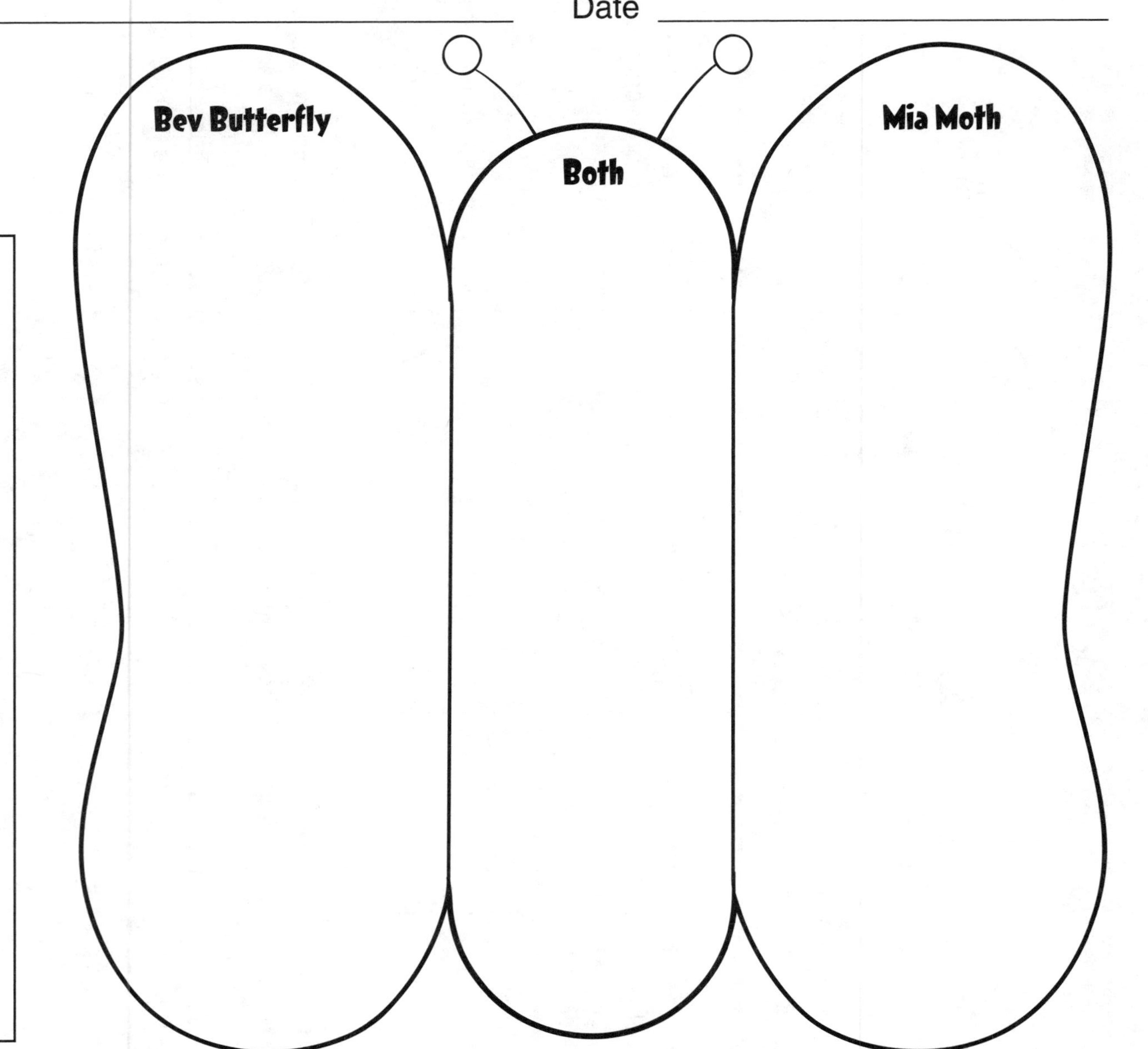

Note to the teacher: Use with page 37.

Sequence

Use with a fiction story.

Name ______________________________

Date ____________________

Choose ___ or more activities to do.
When you finish an activity, color its number.

Title ________________________________

1 Draw a comic strip. Show how the characters try to solve the story's problem. Be sure to name the problem in the first frame and tell how it is solved in the last frame.	**2** Make a timeline to show the main events of the story.	**3** Plan a short skit that retells the story's main events from the main character's point of view. Make plans with your teacher to share your skit with the class.
4 Write a recipe for your story. List the main characters and setting as the ingredients. Retell the main events in the recipe's directions.	**5** Do the practice page "Practice Makes Perfect." 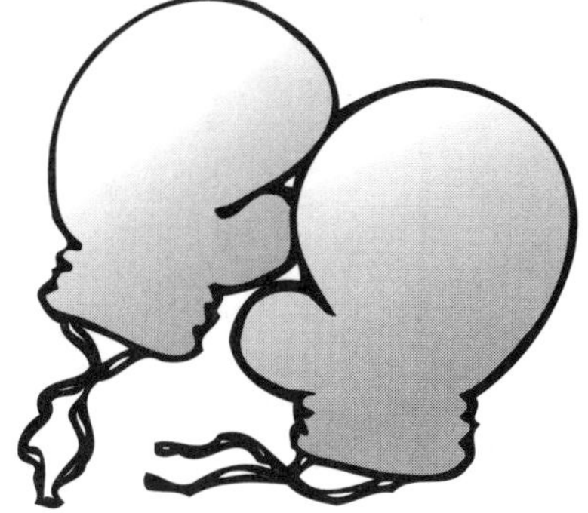	**6** Draw a TV screen. Then draw a picture to show what happens in the story after the problem is solved. Write a sentence about the drawing at the bottom of the screen.
7 Make a list of time order words from your story. Sort the words into three groups: words found at the beginning of an event, words found at the middle of an event, and words found at the end of an event.	**8** Fold a sheet of paper to make six parts. Unfold it. Write in order an important story event in each part. Cut the paper to make puzzle pieces. Swap puzzles with a classmate. Put your pal's puzzle together.	**9** Write the story's title and author on a card. Write about the events in the beginning, middle, and end of the story on separate cards. Staple the cards in order to make a booklet.

Note to the teacher: Each child will need four index cards to complete activity 9. Program the student directions with the number of activities to be completed. Then copy the page and page 40 (back-to-back if desired) for each student.

Name ______________________________ Date ____________________

Practice Makes Perfect

Complete the chart.

Story title:

Beginning:

Middle:

End:

 Note to the teacher: Use with page 39.

Literary Response: Fiction

Use with any fiction story.

Name ______________________________

Date ______________________

Choose ___ or more activities to do.
When you finish an activity, color its number.

Title ____________________________________

1 Write a book review about the story. Use strong words and examples to tell your classmates whether they should read this story.	**2** Draw and label a map to show where the story events take place. On the back of the map, write to tell when the story takes place.	**3** Write a letter to your teacher. Tell about a problem in the story and how it is solved. Then tell how you would have solved the problem if it had happened to you.
4 Make a Venn diagram. Write ways you and the main character are alike and different.	**5** Do the practice page "A Hat Trick."	**6** Make a poster. Draw a picture of what you think the author looks like. Then write what you think the author wanted you to learn from reading the story. Draw a speech bubble around his message.
7 Write five or more questions about your story. Write the answers and the page numbers they can be found on. Use the questions to quiz a classmate who has also read the story.	**8** Copy and complete the sentences. **When I read ____________, I thought, "This has happened to me too." When it happened to me, ____________.**	**9** Write a summary of the story. Include the title, main characters, problem, and solution. Softly read your summary aloud to make sure you didn't leave out any important details.

Note to the teacher: Program the student directions with the number of activities to be completed. Then copy the page and page 42 (back-to-back if desired) for each student.

Literary Response: Fiction

Name ______________________ Date ______________

A Hat Trick

Write a different word from the hat in each box. Complete the sentences.

excited
surprised
worried
disappointed
pleased
relieved

Title ______________________

Author ______________________

Illustrator ______________________

I felt [ ] when ______________________

I was [ ] when ______________________

I felt [ ] when the main character ______________________

At the end of the story, I was [ ] because ______________________

 Note to the teacher: Use with page 41.

Literary Response: Nonfiction

Use with any nonfiction text.

Name ______________________________

Date ______________________________

Choose ___ or more activities to do.
When you finish an activity, color its number.

Title ______________________________

1 On a sheet of paper, draw a picture that shows the main idea of the text. Label the picture. On the back, list three or more important details about the main idea.	**2** Copy and finish each sentence. **I never knew ________.** **I was surprised to learn ________.** **Now that I know ________, I wonder ________.**	**3** Make a word web. Write the topic of your text in the center of the web. Write facts about your topic.
4 Draw a picture or diagram to show details you learned from your text. Label your drawing.	**5** Do the practice page "On Duty."	**6** Write to tell why the author wrote this text. Use examples from the reading to support your ideas.
7 Talk quietly with a classmate about the text. Write three things you both found interesting.	**8** Was this text interesting? Write a review. Use the code and tell why you gave the text that rating. ★ = poor ★★ = fair ★★★ = good ★★★★ = great	**9** Make a list of three new words that you learned from reading this text. Write each word in a different sentence. Use details to show the meaning of each word.

Note to the teacher: Program the student directions with the number of activities to be completed. Then copy the page and page 44 (back-to-back if desired) for each student.

Literary Response: Nonfiction

Name____________________ Date__________

On Duty

Write two details in each section of the life preserver.

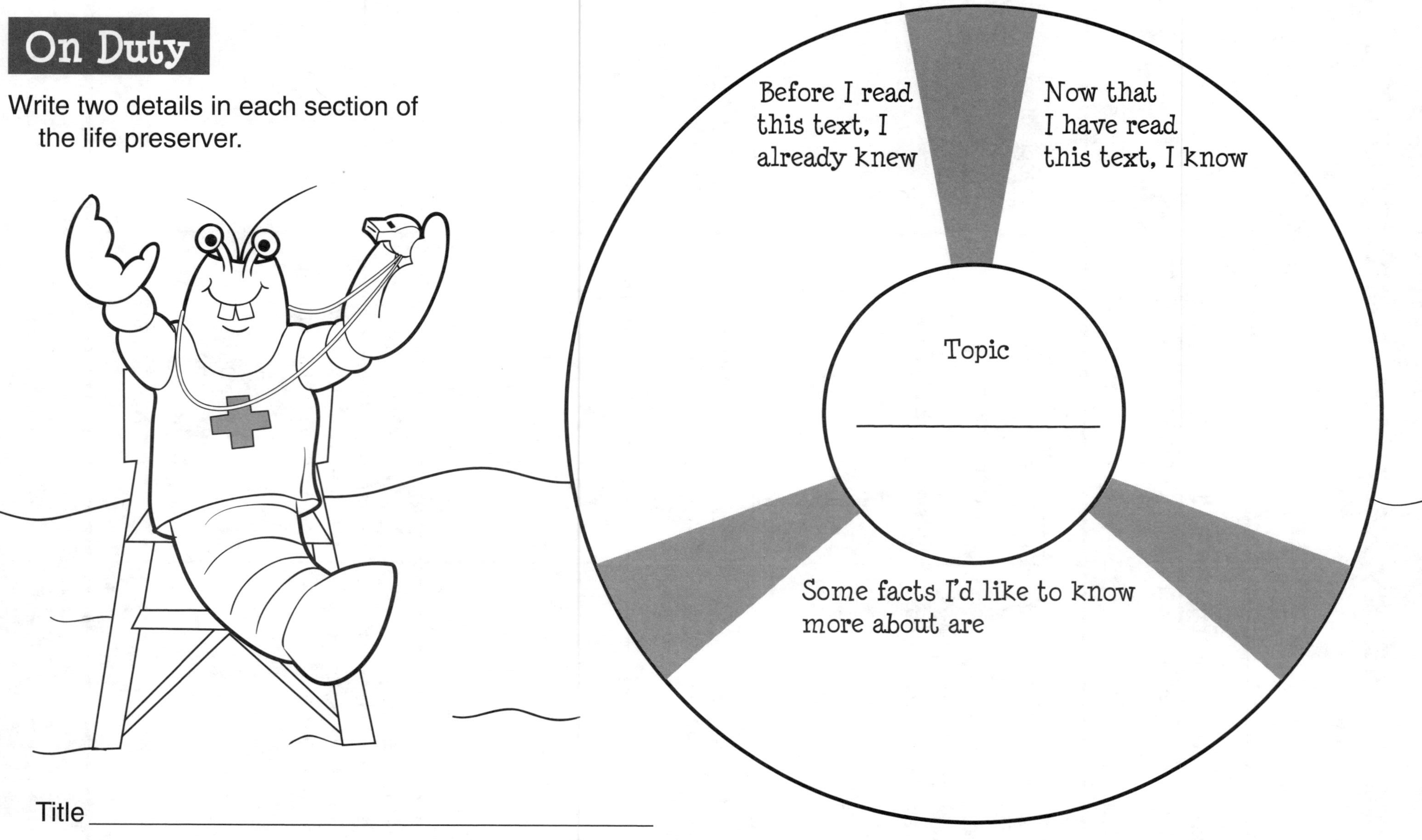

Title____________________

Note to the teacher: Use with page 43.

Compound Words

Name ______________________________

Date ______________________

Choose ___ or more activities to do.
When you finish an activity, color its number.

1 Use only the words below to make nine different compound words. Softly read aloud each word you make.

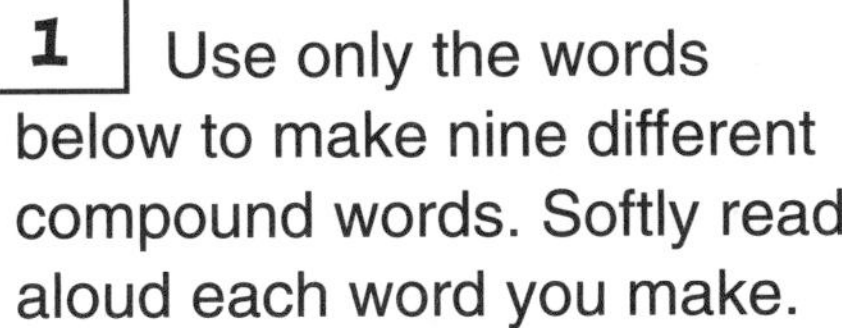

2 Draw picture puzzles for five or more compound words.

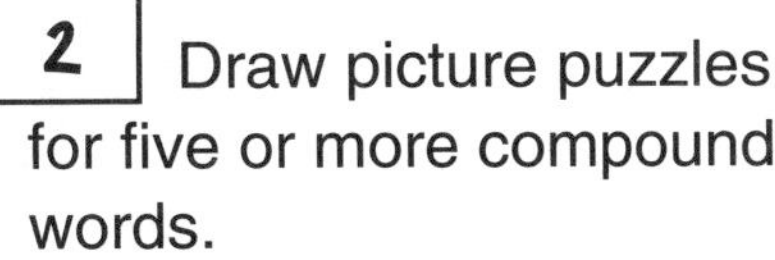

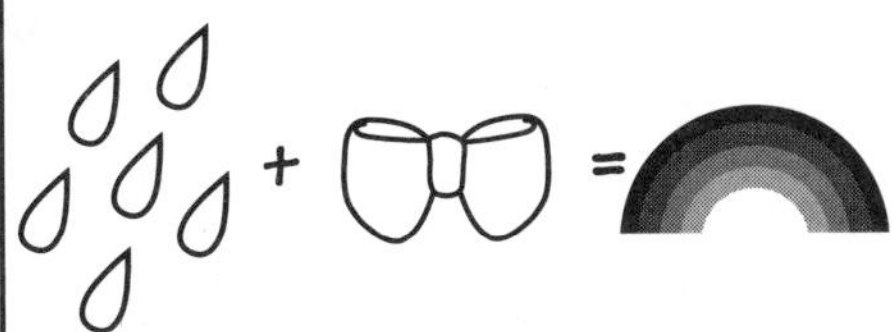

3 List objects in your room that have compound word names. On another sheet of paper, draw a map of your room. Cut out each word and glue it to the map.

4 Copy the sun. Write a different compound word that begins with *sun* on each ray.

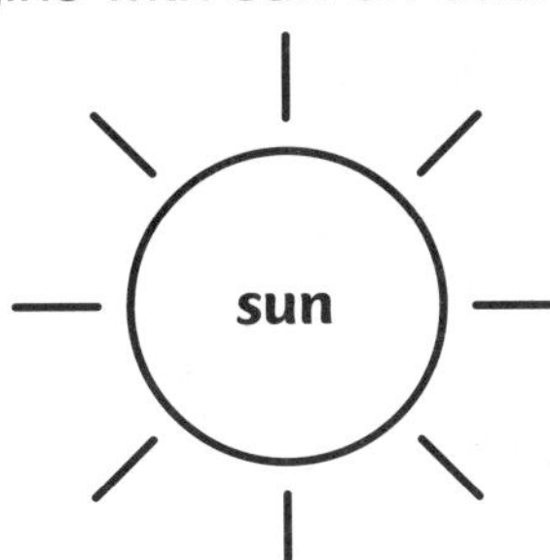

5 Do the practice page "Star of the Show."

6 Write a compound word. Use the second word part as the first word part of the next word. Continue as long as you can.

moonlight
lighthouse
houseboat

7 Write each part of a compound word on a separate card. Use 20 cards. Shuffle the cards. Find the matching cards.

8 Draw a garden. Show plants and insects that have compound word names. Make a chart. List the name of each plant or insect.

Plant	Insect
strawberry	ladybug

9 Use compound words to make eight math problems. Invite a classmate to solve the problems.

cupcake – cup = _____

butter + _____ = butterfly

Note to the teacher: Program the student directions with the number of activities to be completed. Then copy the page and page 46 (back-to-back if desired) for each student.

Compound Words

Name ______________________ Date ______________

Star of the Show

Write a word for each clue.

1. to walk on one's toes ___ ___ ___ ___ ___ ___
2. a common pet fish ___ ___ ___ ___ ___ ___ ___ ___
3. a drop of rain ___ ___ ___ ___ ___ ___ ___ ___
4. water falling from a stream ___ ___ ___ ___ ___ ___ ___ ___ ___
5. a cloth for washing dishes ___ ___ ___ ___ ___ ___ ___ ___ ___
6. a print left by a foot ___ ___ ___ ___ ___ ___ ___ ___ ___
7. opposite of outside ___ ___ ___ ___ ___ ___
8. sad or let down ___ ___ ___ ___ ___
9. a game of jumping over people's backs ___ ___ ___ ___ ___ ___ ___ ___
10. opposite of sunrise ___ ___ ___ ___ ___ ___

Circle each word from above in the puzzle below.
Reorder the uncircled letters to make a compound word and write it in the space to the right.

r	w	a	t	e	r	f	a	l	l
a	g	o	l	d	f	i	s	h	r
i	l	e	a	p	f	r	o	g	s
n	i	n	s	i	d	e	a	f	u
d	i	s	h	c	l	o	t	h	n
r	t	h	t	i	p	t	o	e	s
o	s	s	i	u	p	s	e	t	e
p	f	o	o	t	p	r	i	n	t

Synonyms and Antonyms

Name ___________________________________

Date ________________________

Choose ___ or more activities to do.
When you finish an activity, color its number.

1 Write five sentences. Use a pair of antonyms in each sentence.

The story made me laugh and cry.

2 Copy and finish the synonym web for *big.* Draw and complete a web for *silly.*

big
huge

3 Write and draw six pairs of antonyms.

4 Copy and finish the chart.

Synonym	Word	Antonym
sizzling	hot	cold
	find	
	shout	
	buy	

5 Do the practice page "Making a Mess."

6 Make a game for practicing synonyms and antonyms. Play your game with a partner.

7 Plan an opposite day. List ten things you could do.

1. Eat dinner for breakfast.
2.
3.
4.

8 Write six pairs of synonyms. Explain how synonyms can improve your writing.

9 Write five multiple-choice questions for a synonym quiz. Make an answer key.

1. A synonym for gift
   a. toy
   b. present
   c. box

Note to the teacher: Program the student directions with the number of activities to be completed. Then copy the page and page 48 (back-to-back if desired) for each student.

Synonyms and Antonyms

Name ______________________________ Date ____________________

Making a Mess

Decide whether the words are synonyms or antonyms.
Circle the letter in the matching column.

	Synonyms	Antonyms
1. find discover	T	S
2. hungry full	H	Y
3. run jog	R	E
4. heavy light	G	A
5. past present	I	N
6. wreck smash	O	S

	Synonyms	Antonyms
7. strong weak	A	S
8. catch trap	U	R
9. sleep rest	W	O
10. always never	S	E
11. calm still	C	B
12. alive extinct	J	K

What do you call a dinosaur that destroys everything it sees?

To solve the riddle, write each circled letter from above on its matching numbered line or lines below.

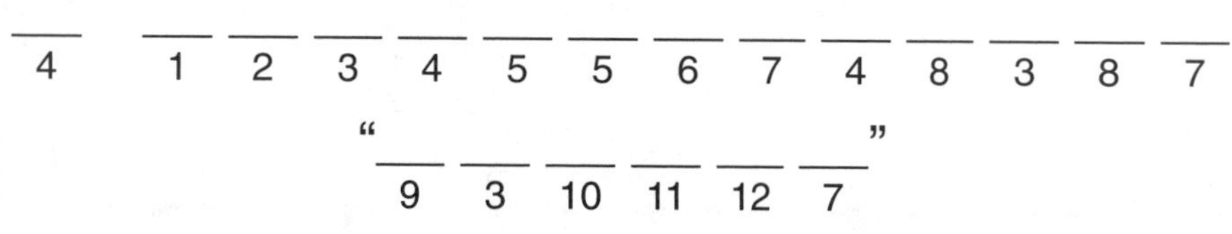

 Note to the teacher: Use with page 47.

Multiple-Meaning Words

Name ______________________________

Date ______________________

Choose ___ or more activities to do.
When you finish an activity, color its number.

1 Trace your hands. Label the tracings. Write two sentences on each tracing to show different meanings for each word. left right	**2** Make a booklet of multiple-meaning words. Put a word and its meanings on each page. Multiple-Meaning Words	**3** Draw two pictures for each word. Show a different meaning with each picture. **nail** **horn** **roll** **fair** **tag** **cold**
4 Explain how you know what the word "trip" means in this sentence. ***My family took a trip to Mexico last summer.***	**5** Do the practice page "Meet Jake."	**6** These words are related to baseball. **bat** **pitcher** **ball** **home** **strike** **out** For each word, write a meaning that does **not** relate to baseball.
7 Make flash cards. First, unscramble the letters in each word. Write each word on one side of a card. On the other side, draw pictures or write meanings. **isnk** **tfee** **prak** **alfl** **eifr**	**8** Ask ten different classmates, "What does *wave* mean?" Make a tally chart to show which meaning was given most often.	**9** Write a riddle for each answer. **a ruler's ruler** **a top's top** **a light light** What item does a person at a sporting event use to cool off? a fan's fan

Note to the teacher: Program the student directions with the number of activities to be completed. Then copy the page and page 50 (back-to-back if desired) for each student.

Multiple-Meaning Words

Name ______________________________ Date ____________________

Meet Jake

Read.

Jake the snake lives in my backyard.
I've tried to catch him, but it's **hard!**
His **scales** are green; his eyes are **gold;**
And, for a snake, he's rather bold.
He has no **feet** to run and **play**
Or to go to the skate park every day.
Jake wears a helmet on his head
And rides around my **yard** instead.

Write a bold word from the poem for each pair of meanings.
Then circle the meaning that is used in the poem.

	Meaning	Meaning	Word
1	12-inch lengths of measurement	body parts at the ends of your legs	
2	tools for weighing	covering on fish and reptiles	
3	a grassy lawn	a length of three feet	
4	a live performance on a stage	have fun	
5	the opposite of soft	not easy	
6	a yellowish color	a valuable metal	

 Note to the teacher: Use with page 49.

Prefixes *un-*, *re-*, and *sub-*

Name ______________________________

Date ______________________

Choose ___ or more activities to do.
When you finish an activity, color its number.

1 Draw pictures to show each pair of words. Label each picture.

load, unload
happy, unhappy
cover, uncover
washed, unwashed

2 Make a bookmark. On one side, copy and complete the sentence below. On the other side, write a meaning or meanings for each of the following prefixes: *un-*, *re-*, *sub-*.

A prefix is found ________ a word.

3 Add *un-*, *re-*, or *sub-* to each word. Then write each word in a sentence.

write	**title**	**fair**
happy	**soil**	**pay**

4 Copy and complete the chart. Use the words shown. Then add two more words to each column.

Prefix	No Prefix

replace	**read**	**record**	**review**
rewash	**really**	**retell**	**reread**

5 Do the practice page "Pastry Path."

6 Plan how you would explain that adding *un-*, *re-*, or *sub-* to a base word changes the meaning of the word. Share your explanation with a friend.

7 Pretend you have to repeat everything you say and do for an entire day. Write about your day. Use words with the prefix *re-* when you can.

8 Copy each word. If *un-* means *not* in the word, trace the word with an orange crayon. If *un-* means *do the opposite,* trace the word with a blue crayon.

unsafe	**unlucky**	**unpack**	**untie**
unkind	**unreal**	**unlock**	**uncover**

9 Write to tell why *sub-* is not a prefix in the word *subject.* Then use a dictionary to find three words with the prefix *sub-*.

Note to the teacher: Program the student directions with the number of activities to be completed. Then copy the page and page 52 (back-to-back if desired) for each student.

Prefixes *un-*, *re-*, and *sub-*

Name ______________________ Date ______________

Pastry Path

Color each space that does not show a prefix and a base word.
In each uncolored space, underline the prefix and circle the base word.
Follow the uncolored path to the baker's finest dessert.

uncle	ready	rent	review	uncover	subtitle
retry	unusual	rest	subzero	resist	subtle
reef	subfloor	subject	reuse	under	relish
real	unclear	recipe	unhappy	red	reach
union	reread	subsoil	reheat	read	subs

éclair

cupcake

cannoli

croissant

cookie

Note to the teacher: Use with page 51.

Suffixes: *-ful, -ly, -ness*

Name ______________________________

Date ________________________

Choose ___ or more activities to do.
When you finish an activity, color its number.

1 Write a list of five action verbs. Next to each verb, write a word that has the suffix *-ly*. Act out each word pair for a friend. Have your pal guess the words.

whisper quietly

2 Copy the turtle shell. Add the suffix *-ness* to each base word. Use each real word you make in a different sentence.

cold **ill**
jump **dark**
sad **write**

3 Add *-ful* to each base word. To the right of each word, write a noun it can describe. Draw a picture to match each word pair.

play **use** **pain**
help **power** **watch**

4 Add *-ly* or *-ful* to each base word. Then write a sentence telling when you might feel or act that way.

kind **cheer**

hope **loud**

5 Do the practice page "Joyfully Jumping."

6 Create a chant that helps you remember the meaning of the suffixes *-ness* and *-ful*. Practice the chant. Make plans to share it with your teacher.

7 Write *sad*. Cut out and label a triangle to match the one shown. Put each corner at the end of *sad*. Write the real words you make. Repeat with *joy* and *soft*.

ful
ly **ness**

8 Write a short summary of a fairy tale. Make your summary more descriptive by adding five words with the suffixes *-ful, -ly,* or *-ness.*

9 Add the suffix shown to each base word. Remember to change each *y* to *i.* Then write the meaning of each new word.

beauty + ful **happy + ly**
empty + ness **pity + ful**
steady + ly **lazy + ness**

Note to the teacher: Program the student directions with the number of activities to be completed. Then copy the page and page 54 (back-to-back if desired) for each student.

Suffixes: *-ful, -ly, -ness*

Name ____________________ Date ____________

Joyfully Jumping

Use the code to write new words.

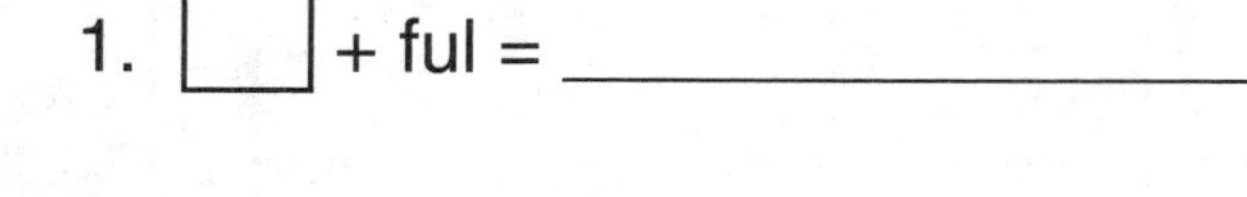

cheer	kind	hope
quiet	help	faith
soft	truth	weak

1. ☐ + ful = ____________
2. ☐ + ness = ____________
3. ☐ + ly = ____________
4. ☐ + ful = ____________
5. ☐ + ness = ____________
6. ☐ + ful = ____________
7. ☐ + ness = ____________
8. ☐ + ly = ____________
9. ☐ + ful = ____________
10. ☐ + ly = ____________
11. ☐ + ful = ____________
12. ☐ + ness = ____________

Note to the teacher: Use with page 53.

Prefixes and Suffixes

Name ______________________________

Date ______________________

Choose ___ or more activities to do.
When you finish an activity, color its number.

1 Flip a coin ten times. Each time it lands on heads, write a word with a prefix. Each time it lands on tails, write a word with a suffix. 	**2** Add the prefix *un-* or *re-* and the suffix *-able* or *-ful* to each base word. Write each word in a different sentence. **place** **help** **break**	**3** Tell a classmate two ways prefixes and suffixes are alike and two ways they are different. Then write a letter to your teacher to explain what you shared.
4 Make a Venn diagram like the one shown. Write three or more words in each section. 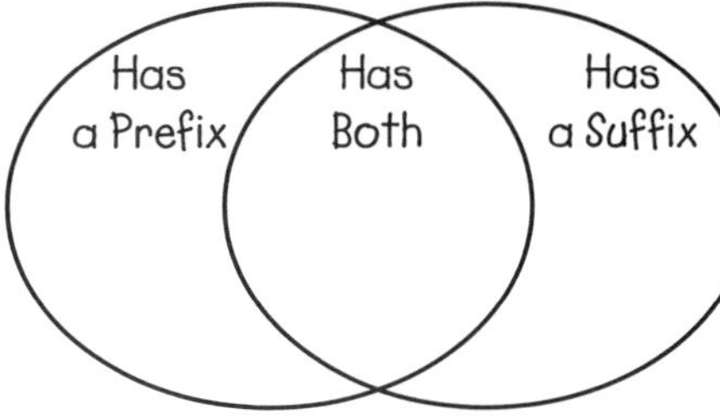	**5** Do the practice page "In the Desert." 	**6** The suffixes *-ful* and *-less* have opposite meanings. Write three pairs of antonyms that use the suffixes. Draw pictures to show the meaning of each pair. careful careless
7 Add the prefix *dis-*, *mis-*, or *un-* to each word. Cut out the words, sort them by prefix, and glue them to another sheet of paper. **place like fold use** **cover obey kind behave**	**8** Make a poster that shows how prefixes and suffixes change the meaning of words.	**9** Read three pages of a story. Write each word that has a prefix or suffix. Make a graph that shows your results. 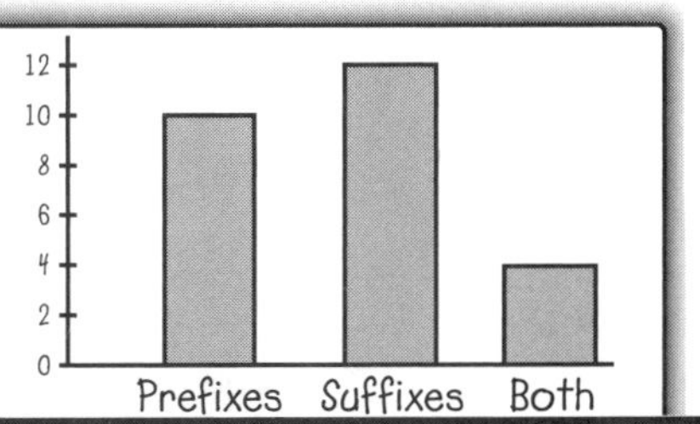

Note to the teacher: Program the student directions with the number of activities to be completed. Then copy the page and page 56 (back-to-back if desired) for each student.

Prefixes and Suffixes

Name ______________________________ Date ____________________

In the Desert

Write a word for each clue.
Hint: pay attention to the base word in each clue to make each word.
Trace each prefix with an orange crayon.
Trace each suffix with a brown crayon.

1. the opposite of *connect* ___ ___ ___ (___) ___ ___ ___ ___ ___ ___
2. not *aware* ___ ___ (___) ___ ___ ___ ___
3. in a *calm* way ___ ___ ___ (___) ___ ___
4. in a *free* way ___ ___ (___) ___ ___ ___
5. full of *help* ___ ___ (___) ___ ___ ___ ___
6. full of *color* ___ ___ ___ ___ ___ (___) ___ ___
7. *lead* the wrong way ___ ___ ___ (___) ___ ___ ___
8. able to be *chewed* ___ ___ ___ ___ (___) ___ ___ ___
9. *judge* before ___ ___ ___ ___ ___ ___ (___) ___
10. *write* again ___ ___ ___ ___ ___ ___ (___)

Why is it hard to see a camel in the desert?
To solve the riddle, write each circled letter from above in order on the lines below.

They are "___ ___ ___ ___ ___ - ___ ___ ___ ___ ___d"!

 Note to the teacher: Use with page 55.

Vocabulary

Use with your own word list.

Name ______________________________

Date ______________________

Choose ___ or more activities to do.
When you finish an activity, color its number.

1 Copy and complete the chart with a word from your list. Repeat with three more words. **Word:** **What this word is:** / **What this word is not:**	**2** Write each word on its own card. Then write each meaning on its own card. Shuffle the cards. Use them to play a memory game. famished really hungry	**3** Draw pictures to show the meanings of three or more words. Explain your pictures to a classmate.
4 Write a paragraph. Use five or more vocabulary words. Highlight each word.	**5** Do the practice page "Reaching New Heights." Cookies	**6** Rewrite the song "Mary Had a Little Lamb." Instead of Mary and her lamb, write about a vocabulary word or two.
7 Make a fill-in-the-blank quiz for your words. 1. An _______ has water all around it.	**8** Write a word. Explain why this is an important word for you to know. Repeat with four more words.	**9** List five vocabulary words. Describe a personal connection you have with each word. bizarre–My brother wears bizarre hats. All my friends think his hats are strange.

Note to the teacher: Each student needs a list of eight or more theme-, story-, or topic-related vocabulary words. He also needs two blank cards for each word to complete activity 2. Program the student directions with the number of activities to be completed. Then copy the page and page 58 (back-to-back if desired) for each student.

Name ____________________ Date ____________

Reaching New Heights

Write a different vocabulary word on each row.
Complete the chart.

Word	Starts Like	Ends Like	Means

Note to the teacher: Use with page 57.

Vocabulary

Use with your own word list.

Name ______________________________

Date ______________________

Choose ___ or more activities to do.
When you finish an activity, color its number.

1 Choose a word. Write down everything you know about the word. Repeat with three more words.	**2** Make a dictionary page for five or more of your words. Put guide words at the top of the page. Write a meaning for each word. Show pictures when you can.	**3** Write each word and its meaning on a different card. Sort the cards into two groups: words you understand and words you don't understand. Then study the words you don't understand.
4 Write a poem. Use four or more vocabulary words.	**5** Do the practice page "What's in a Word?"	**6** Use your words and their meanings to make a crossword puzzle. Have a classmate complete it. 1 2 3
7 Copy the sentence and fill in the first blank with a vocabulary word. Then complete the sentence. Repeat for five different words. Complete each sentence differently. **I might use the word ______ when I am talking about _________.**	**8** Draw a picture that shows the meanings of four words. Label each part of the picture with its matching word.	**9** Copy a word. Find the word in your text. Softly read the sentence aloud. Write what the word means in the sentence.

Note to the teacher: Each student needs a list of eight or more theme-, story-, or topic-related vocabulary words. He also needs two blank cards for each word to complete activity 3. Program the student directions with the number of activities to be completed. Then copy the page and page 60 (back-to-back if desired) for each student.

Vocabulary

Name ____________________ Date ____________

What's in a Word?

Write a different word next to each number.
Write a question using each word.
Then write the answer.

1. ____________
Question

Answer ____________

2. ____________
Question

Answer ____________

3. ____________
Question

Answer ____________

4. ____________
Question

Answer ____________

5. ____________
Question

Answer ____________

6. ____________
Question

Answer ____________

Note to the teacher: Use with page 59.

Sentence Structure

Name ______________________________

Date ______________________

Choose ___ or more activities to do.
When you finish an activity, color its number.

1 On your paper, tell how statements, questions, and exclamations are different. Give an example of each.	**2** Write four subjects with four predicates. Label each one.	**3** Open a book and copy five sentences. Use a red crayon to underline the subject of each sentence. Use a blue crayon to underline the predicate of each sentence.
4 Write three sentences on paper strips. Cut the strips apart to make cards. Move the cards around to make as many new sentences as you can. The / ball / is / bouncing / .	**5** Do the practice page "Penguin in Paradise."	**6** Create a poem. Include three or more questions and three or more exclamations in your poem. Why are penguins cute? They have black-and-white suits!
7 Listen to a conversation at home or school. Do the speakers always use complete sentences? Give examples. Tell why people might use incomplete sentences when they're talking.	**8** Copy the examples below. Draw a star next to the complete sentence. Tell how you know. **Terry picks up a book.** **gives her mom a hug.**	**9** List five questions you would ask a new student. Then pretend you are a new student. Write complete sentences to answer each question. What is your name? My name is Deb.

Note to the teacher: Program the student directions with the number of activities to be completed. Then copy the page and page 62 (back-to-back if desired) for each student.

Sentence Structure

Name ____________________ Date ____________________

Penguin in Paradise

Look at each sentence.
Decide whether the underlined words are subjects, predicates, or neither.
Circle the letter in the matching column.

	Subject	Predicate	Neither
1. Percy <u>packs his</u> suitcase.	P	A	S
2. His friend <u>drives him to the airport</u>.	G	N	O
3. <u>The airport</u> is a busy place.	L	U	T
4. <u>A man</u> checks Percy's ticket.	U	N	I
5. Percy <u>gets on</u> the plane.	O	P	N
6. The pilot <u>talks to Percy</u>.	N	E	G
7. <u>Some people</u> listen to music.	A	S	L
8. <u>The trip</u> is short.	T	L	I
9. The plane <u>lands at the airport</u>.	N	I	E
10. The people <u>smile</u>.	N	O	U
11. Percy's smile <u>is the biggest</u> one.	A	S	G
12. <u>He</u> is ready for a vacation!	P	T	E

What's black and white and lives in Hawaii?
To solve the riddle, write each circled letter from above on its matching numbered line below.

___ (7)   ___ (3) ___ (10) ___ (1) ___ (8)   ___ (12) ___ (6) ___ (2) ___ (11) ___ (4) ___ (9) ___ (5)

 Note to the teacher: Use with page 61.

Capitalization

Name ______________________________

Date _____________________

Choose ___ or more activities to do.
When you finish an activity, color its number.

1 Write the names and dates of eight holidays. Use a calendar to help you.

1. Flag Day, June 14
2.
3.
4.
5.
6.
7.
8.

2 Draw a map of a pretend state. Include five cities, one mountain, one lake, and two rivers on your map. Label each city and landform.

Smith City
Long River

3 Make a list of six places you would like to visit. Next to each place, write the names of two or more people with whom you would like to travel.

England: Helen Bowen and Sarah Bowen

4 Design a party invitation. Tell who the party is for. Tell when and where the party will be held.

Time for a Party!
Who:
When:
Where:

5 Do the practice page "A Capital Letter."

6 Create a chant about one capitalization rule. Make plans to teach the chant to your class.

Capitalize the first word,
the first word
in a sentence,
in a sentence!

7 Make a chart showing six types of nouns that should be capitalized. Give three examples of each.

Holidays Christmas Flag Day Halloween		

8 List the names of five or more of your favorite singers or bands.

9 Make a poster about capitalization rules. Give an example for each rule.

Don't forget the capital letters!
Capitalize a person's name.
Emily Brooks

Note to the teacher: Program the student directions with the number of activities to be completed. Then copy the page and page 64 (back-to-back if desired) for each student.

Name ____________________ Date ____________________

A Capital Letter

Circle each word that should have a capital letter.

Capitalization Code	
name of a person	= ◯
name of a place	= △
month or day	= ♡
pronoun *I*	= □
first word in a sentence	= ◇

july 25, 2011

Dear Mom and Dad,

I am having fun at Aunt penny's house. On saturday, we drove to cherry Beach. We walked on the sand. then we had lunch at The burger Hut. Yesterday Uncle chris and i made cookies. they were so good!

I can't wait to see you on wednesday! Then i will tell you about our visit to the smithtown City Zoo.

Love,
Zelda

Write each circled word correctly.
Draw the matching symbol beside each word.
Use the code to help you.

	Code		Code
July	♡		

 Note to the teacher: Use with page 63.

Punctuation

Name ______________________________

Date ________________________

Choose ___ or more activities to do.
When you finish an activity, color its number.

1 Write five questions you could ask a classmate. Ask a friend your questions and write down the answers.	**2** Make a list of six words that could start a question. Then write six questions. Begin each question with a different word from your list.	**3** Copy the web. Complete it by writing words that might come before an exclamation point. Look !
4 Draw a comic strip with a speech bubble for each character. Write sentences that use different end marks. Where are you going? I am walking home.	**5** Do the practice page "Mystery Mail."	**6** Pretend that the president of the United States walks into your classroom. Write six sentences your classmates might say, ask, or exclaim. Circle each end mark.
7 For each sentence, draw a picture to match. Explain how the end mark changes the meaning of the sentence. **I see a bear.** **I see a bear!**	**8** Write a sentence, a question, and a command about your birthday.	**9** Write five sentences for an end mark quiz. Make an answer key. The boat is blue a. ? b. . c. !

Note to the teacher: Program the student directions with the number of activities to be completed. Then copy the page and page 66 (back-to-back if desired) for each student.

Punctuation

Name________________________________ Date______________________

Mystery Mail

Rewrite each set of words to form a sentence.
Add the matching end mark to each one.

1. uncle to package My me a mailed

____

2. it When arrive will

____

3. to it can't open wait I

____

4. what's wonder I inside

____

5. always sends gifts fun He

____

6. could be Do think alive it you

____

7. Here the truck comes mail

____

8. surprise What great a

____

 Note to the teacher: Use with page 65.

Commas

Name ______________________________

Date ______________________

Choose ___ or more activities to do.
When you finish an activity, color its number.

1 Pretend you will drive from Oregon to Florida. Use your finger to trace the route on a map. Write the names of ten state capitals you might pass.

Salem, Oregon

2 Write a letter to your teacher. Circle each comma in your letter.

August 2, 2011

Dear Ms. Clark,
Thank you for helping me

3 Look at this month's calendar as you write the date for each day.

the first Tuesday
the third Friday
the second and fourth Sundays
the first and second Wednesdays

4 Copy each sentence starter. Add three items to complete each one.

My favorite colors are...
I've never been to...
I really like to...

5 Do the practice page "Heading Home."

6 Write three sentence pairs. Then combine each pair using *and*, *or*, or *but*. Highlight each comma you use.

Math is fun, but I have trouble with fractions.

7 Twelve times each year, the date matches the month. For example, March 3 is the third day of the third month. Write the other 11 dates. Add the year to each one. Don't forget the commas!

8 Write three rules about using commas in a friendly letter.

9 Talk with five classmates. Ask each friend to name three favorite games. Write a sentence about each answer.

Lisa likes to play tag, kickball, and softball.

Note to the teacher: Program the student directions with the number of activities to be completed. Then copy the page and page 68 (back-to-back if desired) for each student.

Name ______________________________ Date ____________________

Heading Home

Use proofreading marks to add commas to the letter.
Each time you add a comma, color a feather.

March 5 2011

Dear Gus

How are you? This winter season has been very long. I left home on October 15 2010. My first stop was Asheville North Carolina. Then I stopped in Atlanta Georgia. I had fun. But I will be happy to get home to Bristol Vermont. I will be there on March 12 2011.

I can't wait to get home! Let's go to the park play tag and have a picnic. We'll pack cheese fruit and juice. See you soon!

Your friend

Gwen

 Note to the teacher: Use with page 67.

Apostrophes

Name ______________________________

Date ______________________

Choose ___ or more activities to do.
When you finish an activity, color its number.

1 Sort the words into two groups: contractions and possessive nouns. Explain how you can tell the groups apart.

friends'	men's
let's	geese's
she's	he's
women's	that's

2 Design a poster. On your poster write three or more important things to know about apostrophes.

3 Use the words to form ten different contractions. Circle each apostrophe.

I	you	we	they	
are	have	will	had	not

4 Rewrite each phrase to use a possessive noun. Write and illustrate a sentence for each noun. Trace the apostrophes with a crayon.

- the collar of a dog
- the robots of some boys

5 Do the practice page "Balancing Act."

6 Talk with a friend to decide whether there is one teacher or more than one teacher in the sentence shown. Write to tell how you know.

The teachers' books are on the shelf.

7 Make four contractions that pair *should, do, are*, and *is* with the word *not*. Use the contractions to write advice for a friend visiting the zoo.

You aren't allowed to feed the animals.

8 Write to describe five people you know. Use possessive nouns to tell about their hair and eye colors.

My sister's hair is brown.

9 Cut out 16 paper cards. Write a different letter or symbol from below on each card. Use the cards to make contractions. Write each word you make.

a c d d e e h i

n o r s t v w '

Note to the teacher: Program the student directions with the number of activities to be completed. Then copy the page and page 70 (back-to-back if desired) for each student.

Apostrophes

Name ______________________________ Date ____________________

Balancing Act

Add apostrophes (') where they are needed.
If an apostrophe was used in a contraction, circle it with a blue crayon.
If an apostrophe was used in a possessive noun, circle it with a red crayon.

1. Hannah isnt afraid of heights.
2. Shes a tightrope walker.
3. The ringmasters voice announces her act.
4. Then Hannahs foot steps out onto the rope.
5. The ropes strength holds her weight.
6. Her poles length helps Hannah balance.
7. Hannah may wobble, but she wont fall.
8. The crowds silence helps Hannah concentrate.
9. Itll stay quiet until she is safely across.
10. Then everyone will clap, and shell bow.

 Note to the teacher: Use with page 69.

Adjectives

Name ______________________________

Date ______________________

Choose ___ or more activities to do.
When you finish an activity, color its number.

1 Copy the web. Write an adjective in each oval. Write a paragraph using the words. bike shiny	**2** Rewrite the sentence. Add adjectives. Then write to tell why the adjectives make the sentence clearer. **The boy walked out of the house and into the snow.**	**3** Design a travel brochure. Draw and write about your favorite place to visit. Use at least ten adjectives. Take a trip to fun Aunt Joan's house!
4 Draw a monster. Use adjectives to describe it on another paper. Then read your description to a friend. Have your pal draw your monster. Compare drawings.	**5** Do the practice page "Driven to Win."	**6** Make a new package for your favorite food. Tell how it looks, smells, tastes, feels, and sounds.
7 Write an acrostic poem to tell about an important person in your life. Giving Retired Active Nice	**8** Make a list of five people, five places, and five things. Write two adjectives for each word.	**9** Use adjectives that end in *-er* or *-est* to compare five items in the room to other items in the room. Write five sentences. The teacher's desk is taller than my desk.

Note to the teacher: Program the student directions with the number of activities to be completed. Then copy the page and page 72 (back-to-back if desired) for each student.

Adjectives

Name ______________________ Date ______________

Driven to Win

For each sentence, write the adjective and the noun it describes.
Color the car with the matching number.
Use the code.

Color Code
adjective tells which one = yellow
adjective tells how many = red
adjective tells what kind = blue

	Adjective	Noun
1. Many drivers have come to the race.		
2. They put on their safety helmets.		
3. Then they climb into their cars through the tiny windows.		
4. The biggest car revs its engine.		
5. A green flag signals the start of the race.		
6. Listen to those tires squealing!		
7. The cars race around the oval track.		
8. The drivers avoid several crashes.		
9. Loyal fans cheer loudly.		
10. The fastest car takes the lead.		
11. Look at the time for that lap!		
12. The winner takes the checkered flag.		

 Note to the teacher: Use with page 71.

Pronouns

Name ______________________________

Date ______________________

Choose ___ or more activities to do.
When you finish an activity, color its number.

1 Copy the words. Draw a fish shape around each pronoun. **me** **you're** **it** **us** **hour** **he** **we** **them** **girl** **her** **they're** **she** **you** **I** **him**	**2** Write four sentences. Use pronouns in place of nouns. Then write to tell why your sentences may be hard to understand. She told us they broke it.	**3** Draw a picture for each word. **yourself girl boy toy people** For each picture, list all the possible pronouns.
4 Write a short story. Use five or more different pronouns. Swap stories with a classmate. Use a highlighter to mark each pronoun you find in your partner's story.	**5** Do the practice page "Gone Fishing."	**6** Write five questions for a pronoun quiz. Make an answer key on the back of your paper. 1. He/They are playing a game. Key 1. They
7 Create a jingle to help your classmates remember the object pronouns. Make plans with your teacher to share it with your class. (Hint: you can reorder the pronouns.) **me, you, her, him, it, us, them**	**8** Make a five-page booklet. On each page write a different subject pronoun shown. Then write a word or draw an example of a noun each pronoun could replace. **he, she, it, we, they**	**9** Draw a picture that has four people and one animal in it. Write five sentences about the picture, using nouns as the subjects. Then copy each sentence, replacing each noun with its matching pronoun.

Note to the teacher: Program the student directions with the number of activities to be completed. Then copy the page and page 74 (back-to-back if desired) for each student.

Pronouns

Name________________________________ Date________________

Gone Fishing

Read each pair of sentences.
Circle the pronoun in the second sentence.
Underline the noun or nouns the circled pronoun replaces in the first sentence.

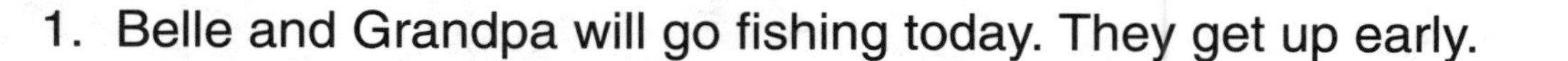

1. Belle and Grandpa will go fishing today. They get up early.
2. Grandma cooks breakfast. She makes pancakes.
3. After breakfast, Grandpa digs up some worms. Belle is not afraid of them.
4. Grandpa carries the tackle box to the river. Belle carries his fishing pole.
5. Grandpa finds a good spot for fishing. It is cool and shady.
6. Grandpa shows Belle how to bait the hook. He is a pro!
7. Then Belle takes a turn. Grandpa is proud of her.
8. Grandpa tosses the line in the water. A few minutes later, he gets a nibble.
9. Belle helps Grandpa reel in the fish. She even takes the fish off the hook.
10. Belle and Grandpa take home six fish. Their dinner will be worth the hard work!

Note to the teacher: Use with page 73.

Adverbs

Name ______________________________

Date ______________________

Choose ___ or more activities to do.
When you finish an activity, color its number.

1 Make a list of five actions (verbs) you can do at school. For each verb, write an adverb that describes how you might do the action.

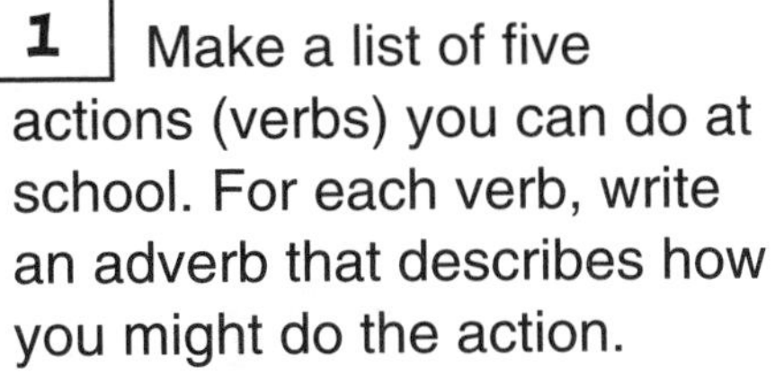

2 Copy the words. Add *-ly* to make each word an adverb. Write each adverb in a different sentence.

glad **sweet** **slow** **rude**
soft **loud** **bold** **quick**

3 Write four sentences. In each sentence, leave a blank for an adverb that tells where. Swap papers with a classmate. Read your buddy's sentences and fill in each blank with a different adverb.

4 Copy the sentence six times. For three of the blanks, write a different adverb that tells when. For the other three blanks, write a different adverb that tells how.

She will do her homework ____________.

5 Do the practice page "Timely Delivery."

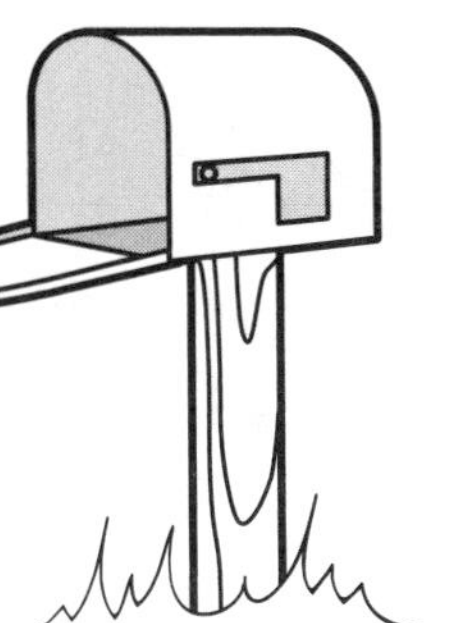

6 Make a chart like the one shown. Add four or more words to each column.

Adverbs Can Tell		
How	Where	When
proudly	here	soon

7 Read. Write each adverb.

The kids play outside. Some run quickly. Others shout loudly. A few girls talk quietly. They watch a boy kick a soccer ball away. Soon it will be time to go inside.

8 Write the adverbs on a sheet of paper. Cut them out. Write a sentence for each word. Glue the word into the sentence.

now **later** **there**
inside **neatly** **sadly**

9 Create a chant about adverbs. Include examples. Make plans with your teacher to share it with the class.

Note to the teacher: Program the student directions with the number of activities to be completed. Then copy the page and page 76 (back-to-back if desired) for each student.

Name____________________ Date_______________

Timely Delivery

Color each envelope by the code.

1. later
2. neatly
3. always
4. here
5. away
6. quietly
7. soon
8. bravely
9. often
10. there
11. well
12. today
13. inside
14. somewhere
15. quickly
16. first
17. slowly
18. far
19. yesterday
20. proudly

Color Code
adverb that tells when = orange
adverb that tells how = yellow
adverb that tells where = green

 Note to the teacher: Use with page 75.

Writing Interesting Sentences

Name ______________________________

Date ____________________

Choose ___ or more activities to do.
When you finish an activity, color its number.

1 Copy and complete the web. Write words that can be used in place of the word in the center. Then make another web for *good.*

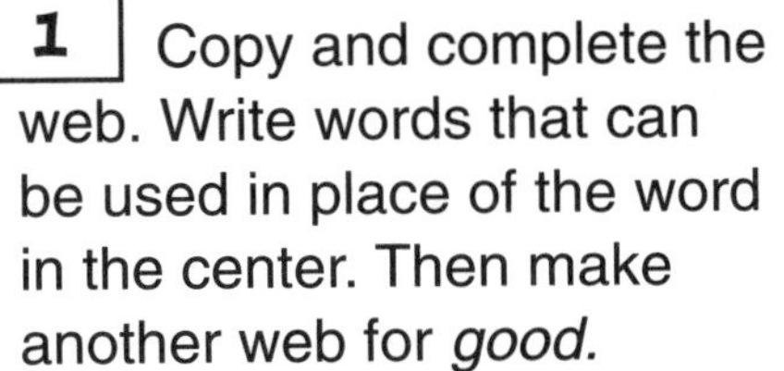

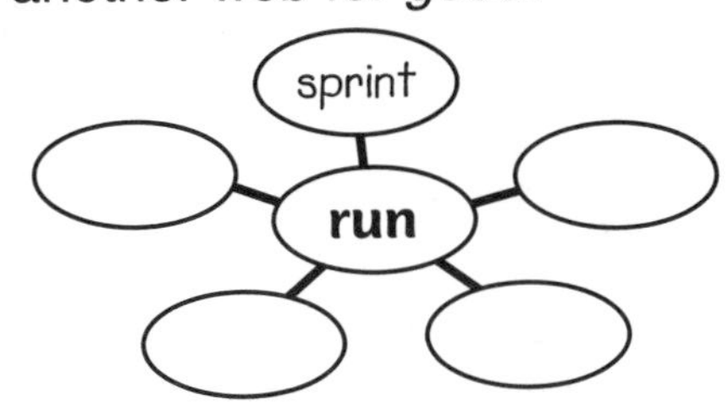

2 List four or more words you can use to join two simple sentences. Use a different word in each of three compound sentences.

3 Draw a picture of a time when you were surprised. Write three interesting sentences that could start a story about that time.

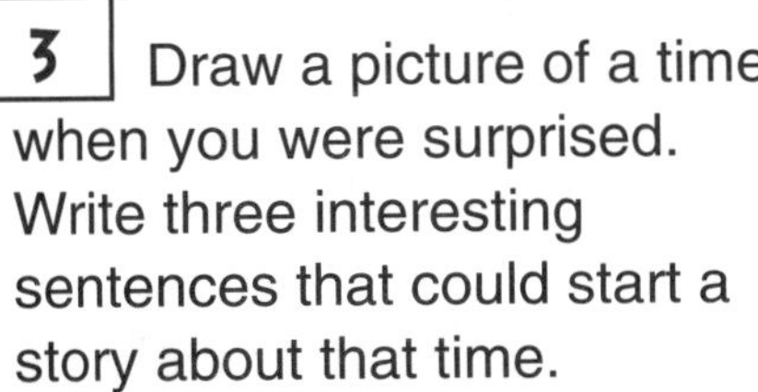

4 Make a four-page step booklet. Start with the sentence shown. Add one detail to the sentence on each page. Draw a picture to match.

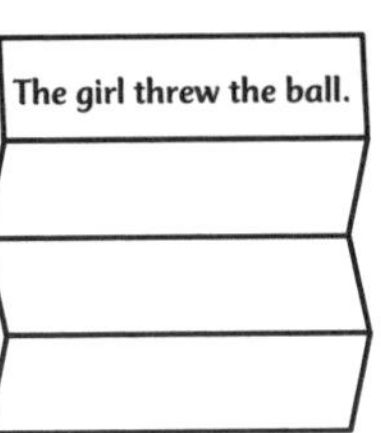

5 Do the practice page "Painting With Words."

6 Use your five senses to describe a birthday party. Write five or more sentences.

7 Make a bookmark for a book that has interesting sentences. Include the book's title, the interesting sentences, and the page numbers where the sentences can be found.

8 Look around the classroom. Write four interesting sentences about things that you see.

9 Write the subjects for six sentences. Have a partner write the predicates. Discuss how to make the sentences more interesting.

Note to the teacher: Program the student directions with the number of activities to be completed. Then copy the page and page 78 (back-to-back if desired) for each student.

Writing Interesting Sentences

Name______________________________ Date____________________

Painting With Words

Write four or more interesting sentences about the picture.
Use the word bank.

____

____

____

____

Word Bank

blazing	strolls	spicy	flutters
crawling	striped	gather	rushing
eagerly	chatting	heats	peek

 Note to the teacher: Use with page 77.

Writing Dialogue

Name ______________________________

Date ____________________

Choose ___ or more activities to do.
When you finish an activity, color its number.

1 Write a conversation you heard today. Use quotation marks. Use a crayon to trace over the quotation marks.	**2** Write a list of words that can replace *said* in dialogue. Use the words to write a dialogue between two friends.	**3** Cut from a magazine or newspaper a picture of two or more people. Think about what the people might be saying. Write a dialogue of six or more sentences.
4 Draw a comic strip about a field trip. Draw three or more frames. Write the characters' words in speech bubbles.	**5** Do the practice page "Early Riser."	**6** Talk with a classmate about a special event in your friend's life. Write a newspaper story about the event. Include quotes in your story.
7 Make a poster about the correct way to use quotation marks and commas in dialogue.	**8** Copy the sentence three times, changing the underlined verb each time. Explain how changing the verb changes the meaning of the sentence. **"I'm not afraid," Jake <u>stammered</u>.**	**9** Write to explain how you know which character is speaking when you're reading dialogue.

Note to the teacher: Program the student directions with the number of activities to be completed. Then copy the page and page 80 (back-to-back if desired) for each student.

Writing Dialogue

Name ______________________ Date ______________________

Early Riser

Write the conversation.
Use dialogue tags and correct punctuation.

____

____

____

____

____

____

 Note to the teacher: Use with page 79.

Writing Tasks

Name ______________________________

Date ______________________

Choose ___ or more activities to do.
When you finish an activity, color its number.

1 Write a thank-you note to a superhero. June 14, 2011 Dear Wonder Girl, Thank you for finding my lost puppy.	**2** Write a poem with eight or more lines. Begin each line with *I wish.* Draw a picture to match your poem. I wish I lived on the moon. I wish I had my own room.	**3** Meet with a friend. Discuss the things you should look for when you edit someone's writing. Create a chant to remember the most important things. Indent each paragraph, paragraph.
4 Write a paragraph. Tell your teacher why your class should have five extra minutes of recess. Give three or more reasons.	**5** Do the practice page "Attention to Detail."	**6** Make a story elements graphic organizer. Plan a story about an alien visiting your school. Characters | Setting Beginning | Middle | End
7 Make a poster about the parts of a friendly letter. Include an example on your poster.	**8** Write a paragraph about your favorite season. Use all five senses to describe the season.	**9** Think of a time when your family was proud of you. Write a story about that time.

Note to the teacher: Program the student directions with the number of activities to be completed. Then copy the page and page 82 (back-to-back if desired) for each student.

Name______________________________ Date____________________

Attention to Detail

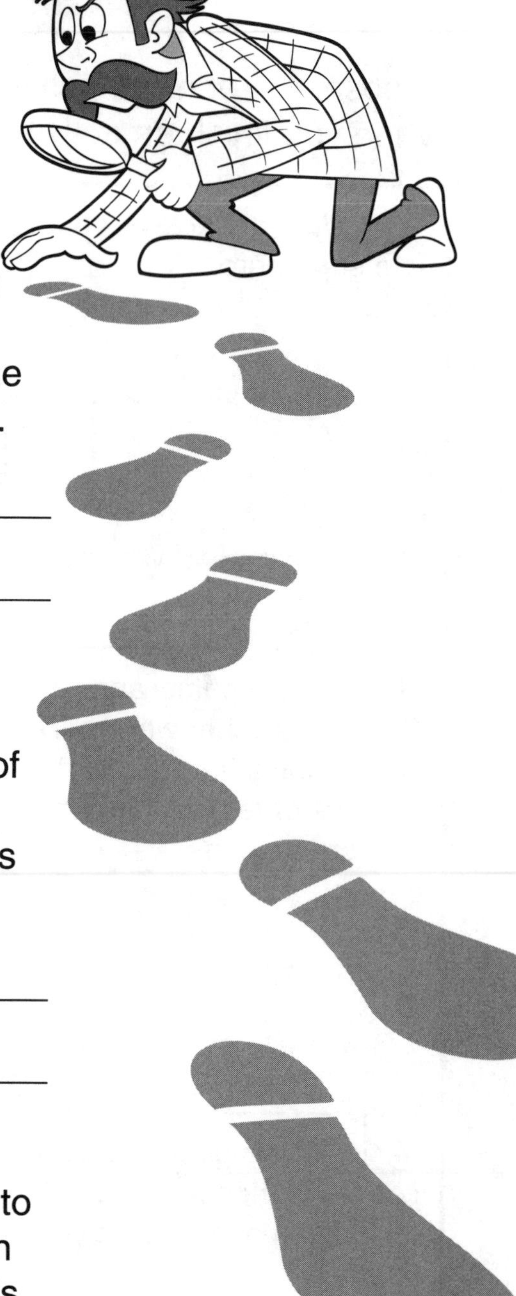

In each paragraph, underline the sentence that does not belong.
On the lines below each paragraph, write a sentence to take the place of the sentence you underlined.

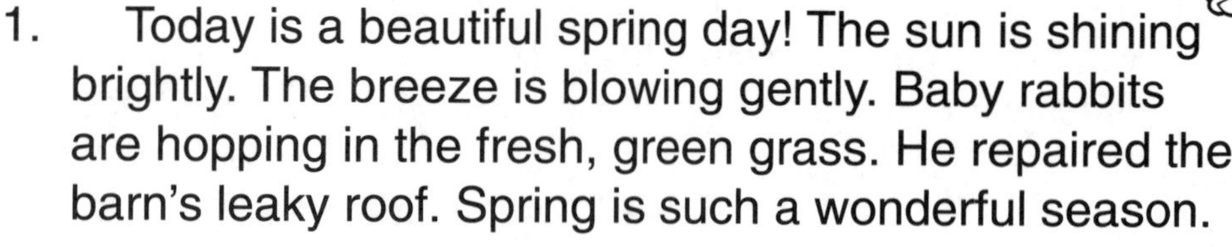

1. Today is a beautiful spring day! The sun is shining brightly. The breeze is blowing gently. Baby rabbits are hopping in the fresh, green grass. He repaired the barn's leaky roof. Spring is such a wonderful season.

____

____

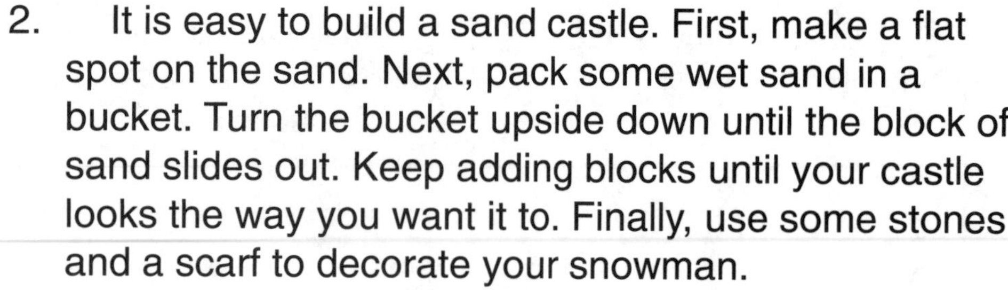

2. It is easy to build a sand castle. First, make a flat spot on the sand. Next, pack some wet sand in a bucket. Turn the bucket upside down until the block of sand slides out. Keep adding blocks until your castle looks the way you want it to. Finally, use some stones and a scarf to decorate your snowman.

____

____

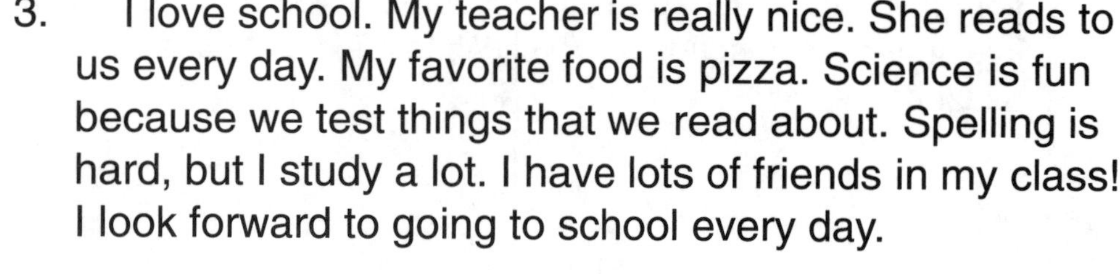

3. I love school. My teacher is really nice. She reads to us every day. My favorite food is pizza. Science is fun because we test things that we read about. Spelling is hard, but I study a lot. I have lots of friends in my class! I look forward to going to school every day.

____

____

 Note to the teacher: Use with page 81.

Writing Tasks

Name ________________________________

Date ______________________

Choose ___ or more activities to do.
When you finish an activity, color its number.

1 Write three sentences that support the following topic sentence: **Funny things can happen at school.**	**2** Convince your parents to let you stay up later on Saturday night. Create a paragraph with five or more sentences.	**3** Write a short adventure story. Write two different endings for your story.
4 Write a friendly letter to a new pen pal who lives in another country. Tell your pen pal about yourself.	**5** Do the practice page "Picture It!"	**6** Pretend you found a secret door in your classroom. Write a story about what happens when you go through the door.
7 Make a poster that tells your classmates where to go to find writing help. Think about the books, people, and places that could help your classmates.	**8** Create a short story with a friend. Make plans to share the story with your teacher.	**9** Write a list of topic sentences for the following subject: **Things I'd Like to Change**

Note to the teacher: Program the student directions with the number of activities to be completed. Then copy the page and page 84 (back-to-back if desired) for each student.

Writing Tasks

Name ____________________ Date ____________

Picture It!

Fill in the chart to plan a personal narrative.

Prompt: ____________________

Main Characters

Setting

Time

Place

The Problem

Details of the Problem

My Feelings During the Problem

How the Problem Is Solved

My Feelings After the Problem

Note to the teacher: Program one copy of the page with a prompt; then make a class supply. Use with page 83.

Dictionary Skills

Name ______________________________

Date ______________________

Choose ___ or more activities to do.
When you finish an activity, color its number.

Dictionary ______________________________

1 Find each word in the dictionary. Complete the chart.

word	guide words
jog	
track	
park	
stretch	

2 Plan a dictionary scavenger hunt. Choose ten words. Write one meaning for each word and the page where it can be found. Include the answer.

relating to dogs; page 56
answer: canine

3 Work with a friend. Create a short skit. Share what you can learn about a word by using a dictionary. Make plans to perform the skit for your class.

4 Look up the word *cold*. Write one sentence for each meaning.

5 Do the practice page "Marathon Runner."

001 23

6 Use your dictionary to find the word that comes before or after each word below.

Before	After
lady	snow
giggle	toucan
pass	baboon

7 Write steps to tell a friend how to find the word *flight* in the dictionary. Number the steps.

8 Find each word in the dictionary. Tell whether the word is a noun, verb, or adjective.

timid **pottery**
inhale **intrude**
cobbler **locate**

9 Write five words that describe you. Which words would be found toward the beginning of the dictionary? How do you know?

Note to the teacher: Provide each child with access to a dictionary. Program the student directions with the number of activities to be completed. Then copy the page and page 86 (back-to-back if desired) for each student.

Name________________________ Date________________

Marathon Runner

Use your dictionary to answer each question.

Dictionary: ______________________________

1 On which page is the word *shoe?* ______

2 How many meanings does the word *run* have? ______

3 What part of speech is the word *strong?* ____________________

4 Find the word *jog.* Write the guide words that are on the page.

______________ ______________

5 Look up the word *marathon.*
Write the definition.

____

____

____

6 Look up the word *stopwatch.*
Write the definition.

____

____

____

 Note to the teacher: Use with page 85.

Informational Text Features

Name ______________________________

Date ______________________

Choose ___ or more activities to do.
When you finish an activity, color its number.

Title ______________________________

1 Describe one of the graphs or charts in your reading. Include the page number. Explain how the graph or chart helps you understand your reading.

2 Copy and complete the chart.

Glossary and Index

Ways They Are Alike	Ways They Are Different

3 Write three things you can learn from the table of contents in your text.

4 Write about each picture from your reading. Rate each one to tell how it helps you understand the text. Use the code.

★ **not helpful**
★★ **somewhat helpful**
★★★ **very helpful**

5 Do the practice page "Come On In!"

6 List three or more boldfaced words from your reading. Next to each word, tell why you think the author chose to boldface the word.

electric–This is a key vocabulary word. It names the main idea.

7 Choose a chapter. Create a table of contents for it. List each subtitle and its page number.

8 Softly read aloud each caption from the text. Tell a friend how the caption helps you understand the text.

9 Copy and complete the scavenger hunt.

Item	Page Number
table of contents	
glossary	
graph or chart	
index	
map or diagram	
subtitle	
bold word	
photo	

Note to the teacher: Program the student directions with the number of activities to be completed. Then copy the page and page 88 (back-to-back if desired) for each student.

Informational Text Features

Name ____________________ Date ____________

Come On In!

Write the matching letter on the line in front of the definition.

A Table of Contents	B Index
I Diagram	L Map
R Glossary	Y Caption

1. ____ a drawing or plan that explains part of the text
2. ____ the words that describe the picture or drawing
3. ____ an alphabetical list in the back of a book that tells which page key words are on
4. ____ a drawing of a place showing features such as towns, roads, and rivers
5. ____ a list near the back of a book that gives the meanings of key words in the book
6. ____ a list of chapter titles and the page numbers they are found on

Which building has the most stories?

To find out, write each letter from above on its matching numbered line or lines below.

The ___ ___ ___ ___ ___ ___ ___ !
4 1 3 5 6 5 2

 Note to the teacher: Use with page 87.

Name ______________________________

Date ____________________

Choose ___ or more activities to do.
When you finish an activity, color its number.

1	2	3
4	5	6
7	8	9

Note to the teacher: Make a copy of this page. Program the top with a book title or skill, and program the student directions with the number of activities to be completed. Write a different activity in each grid space and make a class supply.

Answer Keys

Page 5
1, 3, 6, 8. Answers may vary.

2.
Short Vowel	Long Vowel
cap	cape
bed or bad	bead
dim	dime
got	goat
hug	huge
man	mane

4. Order may vary.
short-vowel words: on, the, bed, one, fell, off, and, his, head, said, put, back, in
long-vowel words: five, the, so, no, three, those
7. Order may vary.
short vowels: red, plum, black, rust, tan
long vowels: peach, gray, rose, lime, teal
9. Possible answers include the following: They are all words with short-vowel sounds. They are all words with long-vowel sounds. Every word can be read with a short-vowel sound and a long-vowel sound.

Page 6

short *a:* plant, pack	long *a:* rain, spade
short *e:* shed, stem	long *e:* leaf, seed
short *i:* wilt, pick	long *i:* ripe, dry
short *o:* crop, sod	long *o:* hose, grow
short *u:* sun, mud	long *u:* tube, mule

Page 9
1–4, 7, 8. Answers will vary.
6. brain, brook, drain, drill, dry, grain, grill, train, trill, try
9. **bl**ends, **dr**aw, **fr**om, **Gl**ue, **cl**ip, **bl**end, **pl**ay, **pr**actice, **fl**y, **bl**ue, **br**ew, **dr**agon, **dr**agonfly, **tr**ace, **cr**ayon (**Pr**ogram, **st**udent in "Note to the teacher")

Page 10

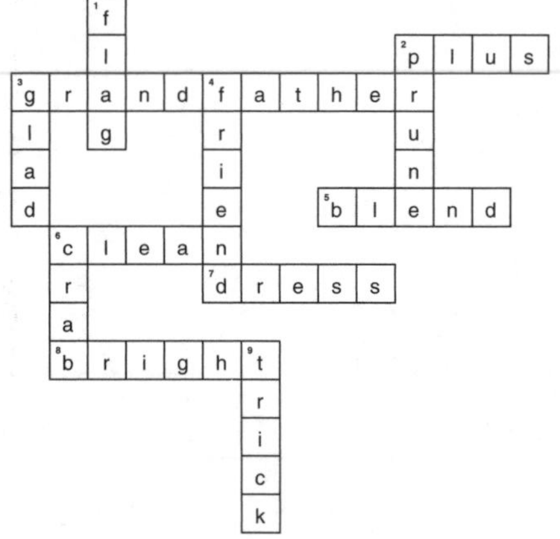

Page 11
1, 3, 4, 7–9. Answers may vary.
2. Order may vary.
spin, skin, spare, scare, span, scan
spell, spout, scout, spill, skill
scold, spy, sky, spunk, skunk
6. Possible groups include words with two-letter blends *(spike, stiff, spend, stuff)* and words with three-letter blends *(spray, straw, stroll, spring)*; words with *spr* blends *(spray, spring),* words with *str* blends *(straw, stroll),* words with *sp* blends *(spike, spend),* and words with *st* blends *(stiff, stuff)*; words with blends that have a *t (straw, stiff, stuff, stroll),* words with blends that have a *p (spray, spike, spend, spring),* and words with blends that have an *r (spray, straw, stroll, spring).*

Page 12

scare	scream	screen	skin	slime
smart	smoke	snack	spoke	spray
sprint	stare	stripe	strong	sweet

t	h	s	c	r	e	a	m	o	s	k	b	s	d
w	s	p	r	i	n	t	r	c	l	s	j	w	s
t	x	y	s	b	d	z	v	h	i	p	g	e	t
r	s	u	c	a	f	l	q	r	m	o	c	e	r
s	m	a	r	t	s	w	l	u	e	k	a	t	i
t	o	z	e	l	l	g	s	o	v	e	r	s	p
r	k	n	e	d	s	s	t	q	c	e	h	t	e
o	e	s	n	a	c	k	i	w	u	m	p	a	x
n	h	w	j	v	a	i	n	y	x	c	b	r	p
g	a	c	y	s	r	n	s	e	k	f	j	e	o
r	z	t	k	n	e	l	u	m	s	p	r	a	y

Page 14
shade, chain, while, which, shirt, whiskers, thought, thumb, white, cheek

Order may vary.

ch	sh
chain	shade
cheek	shirt
church	crush
lunch	fresh
reach	leash

th	wh
thought	while
thumb	which
booth	whiskers
earth	white

booth, church, crush, earth, fresh, leash, lunch, reach

Page 15
2, 3, 6, 7, 9. Answers may vary.
1.
oi	oy
choice	soybean
point	toys
spoil	royal
avoid	cowboy

4.
au		aw	
caught	autumn	straw	laws
August	auto	hawk	draw
vault	because	claw	yawn

8.
BR powder	BR shower	snout
BR down	trout	cloud
BR flower	bounce	BR crowd

Page 16
bloom, football, enjoy, cookie, voice, book, boiler, wood, loyal, soil, root, toys, destroy, oil, droop, noon

Order may vary.

oo like *boot*	oi
bloom	voice
root	soil
noon	oil
droop	boiler

oo like *good*	oy
football	enjoy
cookie	loyal
book	toys
wood	destroy

Page 17
1–4, 7, 9. Answers may vary.
6. *bait, made* or *maid, mate, pale* or *pail, paid, gale, cape, tape main* or *mane, fate, laid, raid*
8. spy tie why
fly lie pie
try by die

Page 18
1. tray, try
2. pie, pain
3. mane, nine
4. sail, trail
5. hay, high
6. knight, knife
7. dice, face
8. fries, fry

Page 19
1, 2, 6–9. Answers may vary.
3. *mope, neat, coat, seat, hope teen, goat, reed* or *read, cope, feed*
4. The following words should be traced in green: *very, every, dirty, sorry, baby, family, study.*

Page 20

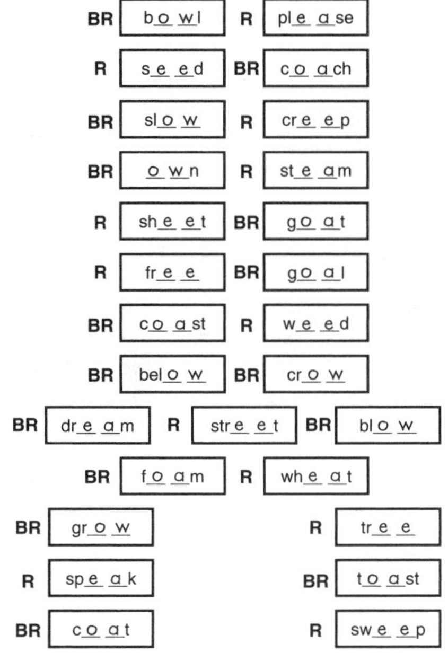

Page 21
1, 3, 4, 7–9. Answers may vary.
2.

Base Word	Past	Present
rain	rained	is raining
wash	washed	is washing
learn	learned	is learning
clean	cleaned	is cleaning
spell	spelled	is spelling

6. brush color ~~eat~~ ~~say~~
~~find~~ fold ~~know~~ walk
laugh ~~see~~ ~~sing~~ ~~think~~
play ~~sleep~~ snow ~~buy~~

Page 22
1. turning (red)
2. writing (blue)
3. batted (yellow)
4. planted (red)
5. swimming (yellow)
6. singing (red)
7. hoping (blue)
8. typed (blue)
9. lifted (red)
10. sitting (yellow)
11. looked (red)
12. thinking (red)
13. driving (blue)
14. winning (yellow)
15. closed (blue)
16. walked (red)

Page 23
1–3, 7. Answers may vary.
4. *Children* means more than one child.
Men means more than one man.
Mice means more than one mouse.
Teeth means more than one tooth.
People means more than one person.
Feet means more than one foot.
Women means more than one woman.
Sheep means one or more than one sheep.
Deer means one or more than one deer.
6. If there is a vowel before the final *y,* add an *s.* If there is a consonant before the final *y*, change the *y* to *i* and add *es.*
8. foxes, cars, pens, balls, dresses, cats, dishes, homes, bags, buses, peaches, boxes
9. Change the *f* to a *v* and add *es.* elves, halves, leaves, shelves, scarves, thieves

Page 24
Order may vary.

Add *s.*
seals
bears
penguins
horses

Add *es.*
foxes
finches
ostriches

Change *y* to *i* and add *es.*
bunnies
ponies

Change *f* to *v* and add *es.*
wolves
calves

Make an irregular plural.
deer
mice
geese

Page 25
1–4, 7, 8. Answers may vary.
6. I see some ants by our blue flowers.
9. *weave; weal, wheal,* or *wheel; weed; their* or *there; your* or *yore; aisle* or *isle; whose*

Page 26
1. find
2. for
3. great
4. heard
5. high
6. led
7. nose
8. sail
9. seas
10. tale
11. would
12. you

Have (you) ever (heard) the (tale) of Captain Ruff? He was a (great) and daring pirate. He and his crew (would) (sail) the (high) (seas.) They were looking for fortune. They never did (find) much gold. But Captain Ruff always followed his (nose.) It (led) him to many tasty treasures!

Page 31
1–4, 7–9. Answers will vary.

6. Answers may vary but should include that knowing that the details support the main idea while the main idea is the topic of the story or passage may help the reader better understand the text.

Page 33
1, 3, 4, 6–9. Answers may vary.

2. *The cheetah is the fastest land animal.* fact; This sentence is always true.
   A cheetah has beautiful fur. opinion; Not everyone would feel that this sentence is true.

Page 34

	Fact	Opinion
1. Cheetahs are the finest wildcats.	Y	A (shaded)
2. Cheetahs live mainly in the African grasslands.	L (shaded)	B
3. A cheetah's spots help it hide in tall, dry grass.	N (shaded)	Q
4. A cheetah can run up to 70 miles per hour.	E (shaded)	J
5. Male cheetahs live by themselves or with a small group.	G (shaded)	U
6. It is thrilling to watch a cheetah chase its prey!	X	S (shaded)
7. Cheetahs have sharp eyesight.	O (shaded)	K
8. Most cheetah mothers have three to five cubs in each litter.	H (shaded)	I
9. Cheetah cubs are so cute!	C	Z (shaded)
10. There may only be about 12,000 cheetahs left in the wild.	R (shaded)	D
11. People should take better care of the cheetahs' home.	V	T (shaded)
12. It would be sad if cheetahs were extinct.	W	P (shaded)

<u>ANTELOPES</u>, <u>GAZELLES</u>, and <u>HARES</u>

Page 36

Cause	Effect
The museum is closed.	We are going to the zoo.
My brother likes tigers.	We go to see the cats first.
It is hot.	The elephants are spraying themselves with water.
We brought our lunches.	We have a picnic.
It is time to feed the seals.	A crowd gathers to watch.
Some monkeys are doing tricks.	We hear a group of children laughing.

Page 38
Answers may vary.

<u>Bev Butterfly</u>	<u>Both</u>	<u>Mia Moth</u>
flies during the day	are flying insects	flies at night
has a slim body	have two pairs of wings that are covered with scales	has a plump body
has knobs at the ends of her antennae	pollinate flowers	does not have knobs at the ends of her antennae
rests with her wings up		rests with her wings spread flat

Page 45

2, 3, 6–9. Answers may vary.

1. Order may vary.
   anybody
   anything
   anywhere
   everybody
   everything
   everywhere
   somebody
   something
   somewhere
4. Possible answers include the following: sunshine, sunlight, sunrise, sunset, sunburn, sunscreen, sunspot, Sunday, sundial, sunflower, sundress, sunshade, sunroof, sunroom, sunstroke, suntan.

Page 46

1. tiptoe
2. goldfish
3. raindrop
4. waterfall
5. dishcloth
6. footprint
7. inside
8. upset
9. leapfrog
10. sunset

r	w	a	t	e	r	f	a	l	l
a	g	o	l	d	f	i	s	h	r
i	l	e	a	p	f	r	o	g	s
n	i	n	s	i	d	e	a	f	u
d	i	s	h	c	l	o	t	h	n
r	t	h	t	i	p	t	o	e	s
o	s	s	i	u	p	s	e	t	e
p	f	o	o	t	p	r	i	n	t

starfish

Page 48

	Synonyms	Antonyms
1. find / discover	(T)	S
2. hungry / full	H	(Y)
3. run / jog	(R)	E
4. heavy / light	G	(A)
5. past / present	I	(N)
6. wreck / smash	(O)	S

	Synonyms	Antonyms
7. strong / weak	A	(S)
8. catch / trap	(U)	R
9. sleep / rest	(W)	O
10. always / never	S	(E)
11. calm / still	(C)	B
12. alive / extinct	J	(K)

A TYRANNOSAURUS "WRECKS"

Page 49

1–3, 8, 9. Answers may vary.

4. Answers may vary but should include that the sentence refers to the family going to Mexico.
6. Definitions may vary. Possible answers include the following: *bat*—a flying mammal; *pitcher*—a jug with one handle; *ball*—a formal dance; *home*—the place where a person lives; *strike*—to stop working or to start a fire; *out*—at the end or away from a place.
7. unscrambled words: sink, feet, park, fall, fire

Page 50

	Meaning	Meaning	Word
1	12-inch lengths of measurement	(body parts at the ends of your legs)	feet
2	tools for weighing	(covering on fish and reptiles)	scales
3	(a grassy lawn)	a length of three feet	yard
4	a live performance on a stage	(have fun)	play
5	the opposite of soft	(not easy)	hard
6	(a yellowish color)	a valuable metal	gold

Page 51

1, 6, 7, 9. Answers may vary.

2. A prefix is found <u>in front of</u> a word.
   un-: not, the opposite of
   re-: again
   sub-: below
3. rewrite, subtitle, unfair, unhappy, subsoil, repay
   Sentences will vary.
4. | <u>Prefix</u> | <u>No Prefix</u> |
   |---|---|
   | replace | read |
   | review | record |
   | rewash | really |
   | retell | |
   | reread | |
8. unsafe, unlucky, unkind, unreal (orange)
   unpack, untie, unlock, uncover (blue)

Page 52

uncle	ready	rent	re(view)	un(cover)	sub(title)	→ éclair
re(try)	un(usual)	rest	sub(zero)	resist	subtle	cupcake
reef	sub(floor)	subject	re(use)	under	relish	cannoli
real	un(clear)	recipe	un(happy)	red	reach	croissant
union	re(read)	sub(soil)	re(heat)	read	subs	cookie

Page 53

1, 3, 4, 6, 8. Answers may vary.

2. Words to use in sentences include *coldness, darkness, illness,* and *sadness.* Sentences will vary.
7. sadness, sadly, joyful, softness, softly
9. beautiful = full of beauty
   happily = in a happy way
   emptiness = state of being empty
   pitiful = deserving pity
   steadily = in a steady way
   laziness = state of being lazy

Page 54

1. helpful
2. kindness
3. quietly
4. hopeful
5. softness
6. cheerful
7. weakness
8. softly
9. faithful
10. kindly
11. truthful
12. quietness

Page 55

1, 3, 4, 6, 8, 9. Answers may vary.

2. replaceable, unhelpful, unbreakable
   Sentences will vary.
7. Order may vary.

dis-	*mis-*	*un-*
dislike	misplace	unlike
discover	misuse	unfold
disobey	misbehave	unkind
displace		uncover
disuse		

Page 56

1. disconnect (orange)
2. unaware (orange)
3. calmly (brown)
4. freely (brown)
5. helpful (brown)
6. colorful (brown)
7. mislead (orange)
8. chewable (brown)
9. prejudge (orange)
10. rewrite (orange)

They are "camel-flaged"!

Page 61

2–4, 6, 7, 9. Answers may vary.

1. Statements tell something. Questions ask something. Exclamations tell something that is important or exciting.
8. "Terry picks up a book."★ It has a subject and a predicate. "gives her mom a hug" is an incomplete sentence. It only has a predicate.

Page 62

	Subject	Predicate	Neither
1. Percy packs his suitcase.	P	A	(S)
2. His friend drives him to the airport.	G	(N)	O
3. The airport is a busy place.	(L)	U	T
4. A man checks Percy's ticket.	(U)	N	I
5. Percy gets on the plane.	O	P	(N)
6. The pilot talks to Percy.	N	(E)	G
7. Some people listen to music.	(A)	S	L
8. The trip is short.	(T)	L	I
9. The plane lands at the airport.	N	(I)	E
10. The people smile.	N	(O)	U
11. Percy's smile is the biggest one.	A	S	(G)
12. He is ready for a vacation!	(P)	T	E

A LOST PENGUIN

Page 64

july 25, 2011

Dear Mom and Dad,

I am having fun at Aunt penny's house. On saturday, we drove to cherry Beach. We walked on the sand. then we had lunch at The burger Hut. Yesterday Uncle chris and i made cookies. they were so good!

I can't wait to see you on wednesday! Then i will tell you about our visit to the smithtown City Zoo.

Love,
Zelda

	Code		Code
July	♡	Chris	○
Penny's	○	I	□
Saturday	♡	They	◇
Cherry	△	Wednesday	♡
Then	◇	I	□
Burger	△	Smithtown	△

Page 66

1. My uncle mailed a package to me.
2. When will it arrive?
3. I can't wait to open it!
4. I wonder what's inside.
5. He always sends fun gifts.
6. Do you think it could be alive?
7. Here comes the mail truck.
8. What a great surprise!

Page 67
1–4, 6, 9. Answers may vary.
7. Year may vary.
January 1, 2011
February 2, 2011
April 4, 2011
May 5, 2011
June 6, 2011
July 7, 2011
August 8, 2011
September 9, 2011
October 10, 2011
November 11, 2011
December 12, 2011
8. Answers may vary. Possible answers include the following:
Use a comma between the date and the year.
Use a comma after the greeting.
Use a comma after the closing.

Page 68

March 5, 2011

Dear Gus,

How are you? This winter season has been very long. I left home on October 15, 2010. My first stop was Asheville, North Carolina. Then I stopped in Atlanta, Georgia. I had fun. But I will be happy to get home to Bristol, Vermont. I will be there on March 12, 2011.

I can't wait to get home! Let's go to the park, play tag, and have a picnic. We'll pack cheese, fruit, and juice. See you soon!

Your friend,
Gwen

Page 69
2, 4, 6–8. Answers may vary.
1. contractions: let's, she's, he's, that's
possessive nouns: friends', men's, geese's, women's
Each contraction can be changed into a noun and a verb. The possessive nouns cannot.
3. Answers may vary. Possible answers include *I've, I'll, I'd, you're, you've, you'll, you'd, we're, we've, we'll, we'd, they're, they've, they'll, they'd, aren't, haven't, won't,* and *hadn't.*
9. Answers may vary. Possible answers include *aren't, can't, didn't, doesn't, hadn't, hasn't, haven't, he'd, he's, I'd, I've, she'd, wasn't, we're, weren't, we'd, we've,* and *won't.*

Page 70
1. Hannah isn't afraid of heights. (blue)
2. She's a tightrope walker. (blue)
3. The ringmaster's voice announces her act. (red)
4. Then Hannah's foot steps out onto the rope. (red)
5. The rope's strength holds her weight. (red)
6. The pole's length helps her balance. (red)
7. Hannah may wobble, but she won't fall. (blue)
8. The crowd's silence helps Hannah concentrate. (red)
9. It'll stay quiet until she is safely across. (blue)
10. Then everyone will clap, and she'll bow. (blue)

Page 72

	Adjective	Noun
1.	Many	drivers
2.	safety	helmets
3.	tiny	windows
4.	biggest	car
5.	green	flag
6.	those	tires
7.	oval	track
8.	several	crashes
9.	Loyal	fans
10.	fastest	car
11.	that	lap
12.	checkered	flag

Page 73
2, 4, 6–9. Answers may vary.
1. The following words should have fish outlines: *me, it, us, he, we, them, her, she, you, I,* and *him.*
3. yourself: I, me
girl: she, her, hers
boy: he, him, his
toy: it, its
people: they, them, we, us, our

Page 74
1. Belle and Grandpa will go fishing today. They get up early.
2. Grandma cooks breakfast. She makes pancakes.
3. After breakfast, Grandpa digs up some worms. Belle is not afraid of them.
4. Grandpa carries the tackle box to the river. Belle carries his fishing pole.
5. Grandpa finds a good spot for fishing. It is cool and shady.
6. Grandpa shows Belle how to bait the hook. He is a pro!
7. Then Belle takes a turn. Grandpa is proud of her.
8. Grandpa tosses the line in the water. A few minutes later, he gets a nibble.
9. Belle helps Grandpa reel in the fish. She even takes the fish off the hook.
10. Belle and Grandpa take home six fish. Their dinner will be worth the hard work!

Page 75
1–4, 6, 8, 9. Answers may vary.
7. outside, quickly, loudly, quietly, away, soon, inside

Page 76

1. orange	2. yellow	3. orange	4. green
5. green	6. yellow	7. orange	8. yellow
9. orange	10. green	11. yellow	12. orange
13. green	14. green	15. yellow	16. orange
17. yellow	18. green		
19. orange	20. yellow		

Page 77
3, 4, 6–9. Answers may vary.
1. Answers may vary. Possible answers for *run* include the following: *jog, dash, scurry, rush, dart,* and *hurry.* Possible answers for *good* include the following: *nice, lovely, pleasant, able, fine,* and *fair.*
2. Answers may vary and may include the following: *and, but, or, yet,* or *so.* Sentences will vary.

Page 79
1, 3, 4, 6, 7. Answers may vary.
2. Answers may vary. Possible answers include the following: *remarked, called, cried, shouted, yelled,* and *whispered.*
8. Possible answers include the following:
   "I'm not afraid," Jake stated.
   "I'm not afraid," Jake whispered.
   "I'm not afraid," Jake yelled.
   The verb helps the reader understand the character's feelings.
9. The dialogue tag tells you who is speaking.

Page 80
Answers may vary.
"Good morning, Joey," Mom said.
"Morning, Mom," Joey answered.

"Did you sleep well?" Mom asked.
Joey said, "No, a noise woke me early."

"What kind of noise?" Mom asked.
"The crack of dawn!" Joey exclaimed.

Page 82
Students' sentences will vary.
1. Today is a beautiful spring day! The sun is shining brightly. The breeze is blowing gently. Baby rabbits are hopping in the fresh, green grass. ~~He repaired the barn's leaky roof~~. Spring is such a wonderful season.
2. It is easy to build a sand castle. First, make a flat spot on the sand. Next, pack some wet sand in a bucket. Turn the bucket upside down until the block of sand slides out. Keep adding blocks until your castle looks the way you want it to. ~~Finally, use some stones and a scarf to decorate your snowman~~.
3. I love school. My teacher is really nice. She reads to us every day. ~~My favorite food is pizza~~. Science is fun because we test things that we read about. Spelling is hard, but I study a lot. I have lots of friends in my class! I look forward to going to school every day.

Page 85
1–3, 6, 9. Answers may vary.
4. Answers may vary. Sentences may be written for the following meanings: having a low temperature; an illness with symptoms of coughing, sneezing, and a slight fever; not friendly.
7. Answers may vary.
   Open the dictionary to the middle of the *f* section.
   Find the pair of guide words that would include *flight.*
   Use ABC order to locate *flight* on the page.
8. timid, adjective; pottery, noun; inhale, verb; intrude, verb; cobbler, noun; locate, verb

Page 87
1, 3, 4, 6–9. Answers may vary.
2. Answers may vary.

Ways They Are Alike	Ways They Are Different
They are in ABC order.	An index tells where the word can be found.
They list words that are in the book	A glossary has the definitions of words.

Page 88
1. I
2. Y
3. B
4. L
5. R
6. A

The LIBRARY!